CONTENTS

Color Section   5
Preface   33
Why Space Patches?   34
1. NASA Logos   37
2. The Mercury Program   39
3. The Gemini Program   42
4. The Apollo Program   47
5. The Skylab Program   61
6. The Apollo/Soyuz Program   66
7. The Space Shuttle Program   69
8. Space Shuttle Program "Related" Patches   99
9. International Space Patches   103
10. The Future: The Young Astronauts Program™   107
11. Individual Program and Event Patches   110
12. NASA Facility Logos   114
13. Collecting Space Patches   117
Appendices   119
Timeline   121
Index   124

SPACE PATCHES
From Mercury to the Space Shuttle

Judith Kaplan
and Robert Muniz

Sterling Publishing Co., Inc.   New York

Library of Congress Cataloging-in-Publication Data

Kaplan, Judith.
  Space patches.

  Includes index.
  1. United States. National Aeronautics and
Space Administration—Insignia. I. Muniz,
Robert. II. Title.
TL521.K33 1986   387.8′027   86-971
ISBN 0-8069-6292-5
ISBN 0-8069-6294-1 (pbk.)

Copyright © 1986 by Action Packets, Inc.
Published by Sterling Publishing Co., Inc.
Two Park Avenue, New York, N.Y. 10016
Distributed in Australia by Capricorn Book Co. Pty. Ltd.
Unit 5C1 Lincoln St., Lane Cove, N.S.W. 2066
Distributed in the United Kingdom by Blandford Press
Link House, West Street, Poole, Dorset BH15 1LL, England
Distributed in Canada by Oak Tree Press Ltd.
℅ Canadian Manda Group, P.O. Box 920, Station U
Toronto, Ontario, Canada M8Z 5P9
Manufactured in the United States of America
All rights reserved

NASA LOGOS

NACA (National Advisory Committee on Aeronautics)

NASA original

NASA extended vector

Official NASA "worm"

Souvenir NASA "worm"

"I Love NASA" souvenir

MERCURY SERIES

Mercury 3

Mercury 4

Mercury 6

Mercury 7

Mercury 8

Mercury 9

GEMINI SERIES

Gemini Program

Gemini 3

Gemini 4

Gemini 5 (1st official patch)

Gemini 6

Gemini 7

Gemini (continued)

Gemini 8

Gemini 9

Gemini 10

Gemini 11

Gemini 12

APOLLO SERIES

Apollo Program

Apollo 1

Apollo 7

Apollo 8

Apollo 9

Apollo (continued)

Apollo 10

Apollo 11

Apollo 12

Apollo 13

Apollo 14

Apollo 15

Apollo 16

Apollo 17

Apollo СОЮЗ 3 Program

Apollo СОЮЗ 3 Crew

SKYLAB SERIES

Skylab Program

Skylab 1

Skylab 2

Skylab 3

SHUTTLE SERIES

Approach and Landing Program

Space Shuttle Program

STS-1

STS-2

Shuttle Series
(continued)

STS-3

STS-4

STS-5

STS-6

STS-7

STS-8

STS-9 (41A)

STS-11 (41B)

STS-41C

STS-41D

Shuttle Series
(continued)

STS-41G

STS-51A

STS-51C

STS-51D

STS-51E (never flew)

Shuttle Series (continued)

Garn's personal 51D design

STS-51B

STS-51G

STS-51F

STS-51I

MISCELLANEOUS

STS-61A

Apollo 14 (Backup Crew patch)

STS-8

APOLLO COMMEMORATIVES

1st Lunar Landing

Apollo 11 LEM5

SPACELAB SERIES

NASA ESA Spacelab

ESA NASA Spacelab

Spacelab 1

Spacelab 2

Spacelab 3

YOUNG ASTRONAUTS

Original logo

Current logo

Logo

Official Teacher in
Space Program patch

25 Mach ("exclusive club"
for shuttle astronauts only)

INTERNATIONAL PATCHES

ESA

Ariane Program

ESA Giotto Program

Eureca Program

ESA Meteosat Program

ESA Earthnet Program

ESA Olympus Program

French Version STS-51G

International Patches (continued)
Canada

Canadian Astronaut Program

Canadian Program, white background

Canadian logo

Space Team (French Version)

Space Team (English Version)

Canadian Version STS-41G

Shuttle Arm Commemorative

FIELD CENTER LOGOS

Ames Research Center

National Space Tech Lab

Field Center logos (continued)

Lewis

Dryden

JPL

NASA 25th Anniversary Commemorative

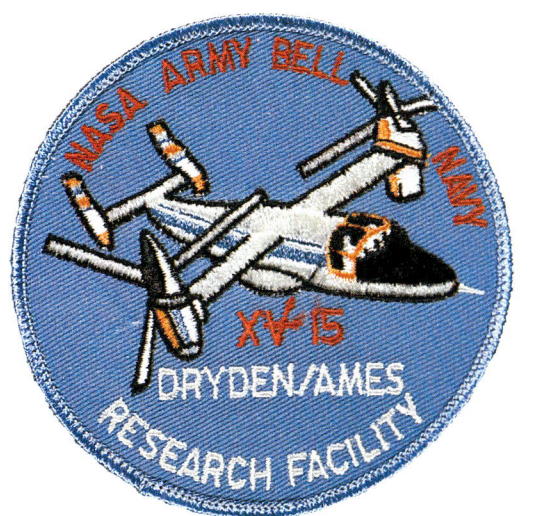

NASA Dryden XV-15 patch

Kennedy Space Center (Visitor's Center logo)

Kennedy Space Center
Fire Department

Lewis Research Center
Official Security Emblem

NASA Wallops Island
40th Anniversary

Field Center logos (continued)
Vandenberg Facility

Miscellaneous Vandenberg patch

Logo patch in military style

Souvenir logo
(knock-off of Dryden patch)

Souvenir

Souvenir of shuttle launch site construction phase

MISCELLANEOUS PROGRAMS AND PROJECTS

Voyager

Viking

Chase team

Shuttle carrier

Miscellaneous Programs and Projects (continued)

Global Positioning System

Tracking Data Relay Satellite System

"You've Come a Long Way, Baby" 3 inches

Manned Maneuvering Unit

Shuttle mid-deck experiments

Office & Aviation Space Technology solar experiment

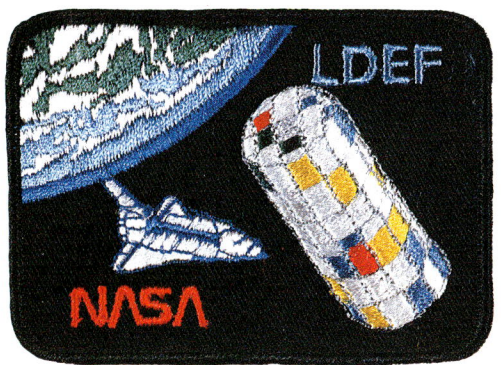

Long duration experimental facility

Galileo Jupiter probe

Outer Space Observatory (future mission)

Miscellaneous Programs and Projects (continued)

Pioneer 10

Chemical Systems Division
Boosters Separation Motors patch

Mission Control

ESA Space Telescope (International)

Grumman Technical Services, Inc.

PREFACE

It is important to note the distinction between the official and souvenir versions of NASA Space Program patches. The official NASA emblems are manufactured in specific sizes. Souvenir patches are often made in sizes which vary from the official, although not always. Great attention is paid to artistic detail and color in NASA's patches. Recent Shuttle mission emblems have had as many as twelve or fifteen distinct thread colors in their embroidery. All this is done in an effort to enhance the beauty and aesthetics of the patch design.

This is not to say that souvenir versions of these emblems are lacking in their own beauty and collectibility. The patches worn by the astronauts and other NASA personnel meet rigid standards for thread color, detail, size, border type and design. Many fine souvenir versions of NASA patches are also available in the marketplace. They are often as attractive as the "real thing," although they can usually be distinguished from the official versions by simple visual comparison. In general, souvenir patches will have slightly less variety in the number of thread colors used. This is usually done to reduce manufacturing costs, thereby keeping the retail price to the consumer as low as possible. They may also vary somewhat in size from official versions. Often, the final look of an official patch differs from the original design due to changes made by the flight crew or other NASA officials. The initial artwork may be designed months before a mission. If changes are made in the flight plan or the crew make-up, this may also cause final designs to differ. Many souvenir versions do not contain these changes, and are produced from the original designs. This usually happens because the public demand for each flight emblem requires that the patch be in the marketplace as soon as possible. To help differentiate the official emblems from souvenir versions, all patches illustrated in this book will be the official ones unless otherwise noted.

Souvenir patches are usually produced to meet the demand for collectible symbols relating to the Space Program. The official patch is manufactured by one or more companies selected in a competitive bidding and quality control process. The patch design and look are approved by NASA and the mission astronauts before the official version is produced. The first emblems "off the line" in production are made available to the astronauts, NASA Headquarters, and select NASA personnel and VIPs. Generally, this amounts to approximately 10,000 emblems.

Once these needs are met, the emblems are distributed to NASA facilities throughout the country where they are made available to the public through NASA Exchange stores and Visitor Centers. They are also supplied to many science museums, planetariums, and observatories, and can be purchased through these institutions' gift shops. In addition, there are a number of commercial, retail companies specializing in space collectibles. These firms make the patches available over the counter and through mail order. Supplies to these facilities account for about another 30,000 emblems. After this initial disbursement, production quantities vary for each emblem, depending primarily upon market demand.

WHY SPACE PATCHES?

Embroidery is one of the earliest art forms. It has been found in Egyptian tombs as well as Incan and Mayan burial sites. It is a very expressive art form, and yet because it is wearable, it is very personal.

The roots of embroidered emblems can be traced to medieval times. Knights were completely covered with armor and the only way they could be identified was by the heraldry crests on their shields.

Times changed and people went from armored clothing to fabric. Shields gave way to embroidered crests, which were adapted to the clothing of the time, whenever group identification was needed.

The military of most countries use patches as a major method of unit identification. Embroidery is the most successful art form because of its wearability, durability, lack of bulk and weight, ability to adapt to any design and shape and reasonable cost.

The development of team thinking was and is a very important part of the training of the military. This is also increasingly true for industry and civic organizations. Many of the early astronauts had been test and fighter pilots and were accustomed to embroidered military insignias as a means of team/unit identification. NASA needed to develop its own individuality, as well as please these pilots. Patches were the best way to do this.

Embroidered patches or emblems are called insignias in the military. Europeans and Canadians call them crests. Still another word is brassards.

The term patch became popular during the 1960's when emblems were applied as "patches" on jeans and jackets by the younger generation. Young people also used patches to promote various causes and identify themselves with particular philosophies and associations.

History of Embroidery

Originally embroidery was done by hand. Embroidery is the addition of stitches onto an existing fabric.

Machine embroidery began in the mid 1800's. Those early machines were able to recreate the hand embroidery with greater efficiency. In the early 1900's paper tapes were introduced to instruct the machine where to put the stitches. Later computers were developed that could create the pattern the machines would follow. The precision of computer technology vastly improved the fineness of detail attainable. Today, the "fineness of resolution" is 1/10 of a millimeter and far exceeds the possibilities of hand-done work, no matter how skilled the individual embroiderer.

The embroidery industry had its roots in Germany, Switzerland and Austria. The embroidery machines were, and still are, mostly made in Germany. In the early 1900's many in the industry wanted some wording to denote the precision and accuracy of the machine method. "Machine-made" was not an acceptable label. The Swiss had a reputation for precision and so the term Swiss embroidery was coined. All the official space patches are Swiss-embroidered.

It is important, however, to appreciate that the art of Swiss embroidery still includes much human involvement. Artists design the space emblems after numerous consultations with the astronauts. Once the design has been finalized, the embroidery firm prepares hand-produced (on sampling machines) prototypes which are approved by NASA and the crew. Most of the official patches are made by A. B. Emblem Company of North Carolina after a careful bidding procedure which weighs the quality and cost and compromises on neither. The ability to manufacture in a timely manner is also an important factor, even though NASA itself will often dictate last minute changes in design. New designs and fast production are also required whenever missions are changed, postponed or cancelled. Highly skilled craftspeople must be involved in the preparation of the computer generated patterns. Once on the embroidery looms, skilled technicians remain closely involved, monitoring the tension of the background cloth and the threads, as well as the registration of the colors. The color of each of the threads must be the correct shade as indicated by the Pantone Matching System (PMS) color number. The length and breadth of the stitches must not vary. A typical space patch has as many as ten to nineteen colors in its design. Compare this to a typical military or commercial patch, which average three to six colors. Any imprecision of color, tension or registration results in a defective patch. Finally, trimming must be executed with a high degree of precision, so that the final appearance is neat, clean and aesthetically pleasing.

As a group, space patches are the finest examples of the quality level of embroidery attainable today. That is due to the intricacy of their designs and the quality of embroidery skill demanded by NASA. As in the space shots themselves, every detail was important and no half-way measures were to be tolerated. To the embroidery expert, they are and should continue to be the standard of excellence.

Quality in an art form such as embroidery is easily discernible to the expert as well as the novice. Most novices will be able, upon comparison, to pick out the higher quality item from its poorer imitation.

The following will introduce you to the most important factors to know to evaluate, compare and appreciate your collection of space patches.

The basic fabric used to produce the official space patches is an industrial weight cotton-polyester twill. All mission and program patches are fully embroidered (the entire fabric is covered with embroidery). They are also multi-dimensional (resulting from building stitches one on top of the other) in order to give the patch additional dimension and enhance its beauty. All official space patches are manufactured with continuous filament rayon threads. These are the most lustrous of yarns usable in embroidery. The official patches follow the original designs faithfully.

Let us assume that you have now begun collecting space patches. You have probably bought them for less than $5 each from stores at space bases, museums, planetariums, mail-order firms, possibly at antique shows, specialized hobby or collecting outlets, or from other collectors. Aerospace contractors often make them available to employees; while the sources are not abundant, they are growing. You are at the forefront of a trend; not following a fad. As space travel becomes more commonplace and programs such as the Young Astronaut Program™, the Canadian Astronaut Program and Young Astronaut of Canada take effect, more merchants will recognize the demand for space related items. Then the number of sources for patches to add to your collection will broaden. Now, you will have an added pleasure in the treasure hunt itself.

Once you have your collection started you will want to decide how to best keep them, display them, cherish them. They are, fortunately, very durable. You can of course wear them on jackets, jeans, or hats (the most common way).

One promotion company in Europe made calendars using the Apollo patches instead of pictures. They were sold to banks and other upscale companies who were assured that their calendars would be admired and appreciated and would not be considered as "just" another calendar.

You can have parts or all of your collection framed. When framed with care and attention, their attractive colors and designs make outstanding wall hangings. Scrapbooks or photo albums, commercially available or made by you, are another way to keep them. By adding a write-up, done by you based on research you do yourself, be it from newspaper articles, books, TV or a trip to the library or bookstore, you put more of yourself into your collection and take more out, too. Consider also setting up a collector's club, so you can share your enjoyment and your knowledge with your students. If you are a teacher, by profession or avocation, you will surely find a source of joy in sharing this hobby with others. If you are a shy person you will be surprised to find yourself overcoming your shyness and talking to others about your hobby.

In collecting space patches, as in the space program itself, the only rule you should adhere to is: do not impose any limitations or barriers to your imagination.

1 ▪ NASA LOGOS

The embroidered emblems of the National Aeronautics and Space Administration have been highly sought after by collectors and souvenir hunters for many years. The patches have almost always been quite beautiful and striking. They were designed to commemorate specific events and projects of America's Space Program. In most cases, the design of the patch is meant to symbolize particular goals, events, projects or ideals. This book will attempt to help clarify and explain the meaning and symbolism of these emblems, dating from their earliest days to the present.

Probably the earliest known emblem that relates to our Space Program is the "NACA" patch. NACA is an acronym for National Advisory Committee on Aeronautics. The Advisory Committee was the first governing body of the National Space Program. It was comprised of scientists and military leaders of the Armed Forces. NACA's logo consisted of a simple set of aviator's wings, with the agency's acronym superimposed upon it. Later, when NASA was formed as a civilian agency of the government, this military style logo was discarded.

The NACA patch is hand-cut into the shape of aviator wings. The border is sewn in black thread in an Irregulier style. Irregulier differs from the more familiar overlock border in that it allows the patch to blend more directly into whatever fabric to which the patch is applied. The background of the patch is sewn in gold thread, completing the military look. NACA is sewn in black thread, as is a shield design in the center of the emblem. The patch is very straightforward, as is normal in a military patch, and depicts no other symbolic representations.

The first embroidered emblem for the new civilian space agency is known, appropriately enough, as the NASA Original patch. The acronym for which NASA stands is National Aeronautics and Space Administration. It is sewn in white thread in the center of the patch. The overall emblem is round, measuring 2½" in diameter. The patch has an overlock border, sewn of white thread. Angled around the lettering of the patch can be seen an ellipse, embroidered in white which depicts orbital flight. The ellipse is angled to point northwest and southeast in the plane of the patch. Above and below the lettering can be seen a number of stars, varying in size. They represent the vastness of space and the frontiers of exploration. A red vector completes the design, wrapping the NASA lettering at an angle perpendicular to the white ellipse. The vector represents NASA's trajectory and direction; thus it is naturally pointed upward, on a heading towards the stars.

The NASA logo retained this look through the early missions of the Space Program. In astronaut photos taken during the Mercury and early Gemini flights, it can be seen attached to their spacesuits just above the left breast. By the Gemini 3 mission a slight design change had the red vector extending beyond the white border of the patch. The patch retained this look until the first Apollo mission, Apollo 7.

The advent of the Apollo program brought about a small change in the NASA logo, which also resulted in a name change, of sorts. The white border surrounding the NASA Original was eliminated. It was replaced with one of royal blue which matches the royal-blue twill background of the emblem. The border is oversewn onto an Irregulier border. The vector continued to extend well beyond the edges of the patch, causing this version to be dubbed the NASA Extended Vector. The extended vector differs from the NASA Original only in one other major aspect: The diameter of the extended vector is 3″ as compared to the 2½″ size of the original. Most collectors agree that, although there is little difference between the two, the extended vector is the prettier and more striking of the logo emblems.

The extended vector logo was designed by the Army Institute of Heraldry. The design was approved by the NASA administrator and by the Commission on Fine Arts. The patch is and was worn by all astronauts, whether or not they wear any other emblems representing their mission. It is usually worn on the left breast. The extended vector is no longer the official logo of NASA or the Space Program, but it remains one of the most popular NASA patches ever produced. It will always be one of the best known symbols of man's journeys into space.

While it is well liked and respected as an excellent design, the extended vector patch does have a somewhat humorous nickname of obscure origin. NASA employees often refer to it as the "meatball" patch. This nickname was presumably invented by an unknown wit who felt that the patch resembled nothing so much as a meatball, covered with spaghetti and tomato sauce (the stars, ellipse and "sauce-red" vector). Be assured, however, that the nickname is always used affectionately. This is not the case with all emblem designs, as we shall see shortly.

NASA's current logo is more modern and very basic in design. It is a rectangular patch, approximately 1½″ × 4″. The border is an overlock style, sewn in white. The twill background of the patch is also white. NASA is centered and spelled out in red embroidery. No other design or symbol can be seen on the patch. The lettering is done in a very stylized, single-line method.

This emblem, too, is now worn by the astronauts on each mission. It is usually seen above the right breast, in the area of a pocket flap or just above it. The patch is known simply as the NASA logo. Like the extended vector, it has also earned a nickname. However, the newer logo is not as popular with NASA employees or collectors. Subsequently, it has acquired the somewhat derogatory name, the "NASA worm." The worm nickname is derived from the single-line pattern of the patch lettering. Observers say it resembles nothing so much as a worm crawling along the ground.

The worm logo may not be as popular as the extended vector, but it is the official NASA logo. The version worn by the astronauts and NASA employees has slightly rounded corners. This version is not available to the general public since it is the current official logo. However, a collectible souvenir version is available. It differs from the official patch only in that its corners are sharp right angles.

A second souvenir version of the worm is also produced in a black and gold motif. In this version the rectangle is formed with a black background and border. The worm lettering is embroidered in gold thread.

The black worm patch was originally designed to satisfy collectors' requests for representations of the official logo. At one time, NASA did not allow any reproductions of the white and red logo, for security reasons. That restriction has now been eased, hence the white and red version currently available. The black and gold worm is generally represented in one of two ways. In the first, the worm is produced in yellow gold against the black background. The second portrays the worm in gold mylar embroidery. Mylar thread produces a bright, sparkling gold that is considered to give a "richer" look to the patch. For this reason, the second version is generally the more popular collectible.

Another souvenir patch that is a quite popular collectible is the "I Love NASA" emblem. While, strictly speaking, it is not a logo patch, it derives its basic design from the NASA worm.

The patch design is a take-off of the familiar "I Love New York" theme, which replaces the word love with a red heart. The patch has a black twill background, formed in the shape of a shield. The border is an Irregulier type, and is oversewn in white thread. I and the NASA acronym are embroidered in white. An apple-red valentine's heart replaces the word love to complete the design.

Even though "I 'Heart' NASA" is not an official patch, fans of the Space Program have made it a popular collectible. Its most common size is 2″ wide × 2½″ high.

2 ▪ THE MERCURY PROGRAM

The astronauts of the Mercury Program, America's first Manned Space Program, wore only the NASA emblem on their spacesuits. There were no official patches designed for each flight; nor was there a Mercury Program patch, as there was for later NASA programs. The Mercury astronauts personalized their missions only by naming their space capsules.

There were six manned flights in the Mercury Program. A research and development vehicle, powered by an Atlas-D booster, was launched on September 9, 1959. This was followed by the first two Mercury missions which were unmanned, and, therefore, unnamed. Mercury-Atlas 1, the first Mercury designated flight was attempted in July of 1960. This flight was designed to be a ballistic-trajectory test of the unmanned Mercury capsule. It was unsuccessful due to rocket failure. Mercury-Redstone 1 was attempted in November of 1960. It was also a test flight that ended in failure when the rocket engines cut out on the launch pad. This led some observers to wonder if NASA was capable of successfully launching a live astronaut. However, in December of 1960, the flight was successfully launched under the same launch designation. Mercury-Redstone 2 was launched from Cape Canaveral on January 31, 1961, carrying Ham the chimpanzee, America's first space celebrity. Mercury-Atlas 2, 3, and 4, all unmanned hardware tests, were completed by September of 1961.

Mercury-Redstone 3 became America's first manned flight on the morning of May 5, 1961 when Alan Shepard flew a suborbital, fifteen-minute mission. Shepard wore the NASA logo on his spacesuit; there was no official mission patch.

He became the first astronaut to name his craft. He chose *Freedom 7* to denote the freedom of the United States and the freedom wrought by man's achievements in space. The 7 was added because his capsule was factory Model Number 7. Most people thought that the 7 represented the original seven Mercury astronauts. The astronauts liked that idea so well that all subsequent Mercury flights carried the 7 designation in their names.

When the Mercury Program ended, a number of souvenir companies and individuals commissioned patches to commemorate the program's achievements. Over the years, certain designs have come to be identified with the various Mercury flights. NASA Visitor Centers and Exchanges now make these emblems available to the collecting public. As a result, they have come to be accepted as the official symbols of those flights.

The Mercury 3 patch is a round, 3" diameter emblem. The border is red, with overlock stitching. The patch depicts Shepard's capsule at the height of its flight path, ready to begin the descent to the Atlantic waters. The capsule is embroidered in silver mylar thread, and outlined in black. It trails three black lines depicting the flight path from Cape Canaveral. Below can be seen the blue Atlantic and Gulf of Mexico surrounding the Florida peninsula. The land is embroidered in light-green thread. A yellow twill background forms the upper half of the patch. In an arc across the top of the patch is sewn Mercury 3 Shepard. At the bottom, in a similar arc is the capsule's name, *Freedom 7*, sewn in silver mylar. Mercury 3 is sewn in the same blue thread of the oceans, while Shepard's name is sewn in the same green shade used to form the state of Florida.

Mercury-Redstone 4 was launched on July 21, 1961. Astronaut Virgil Grissom piloted America's second suborbital mission during its fifteen-minute flight. Like Shepard before him, Grissom wore only the NASA insignia on his space suit. Grissom named his capsule *Liberty Bell 7* because the Mercury capsules were shaped much like bells. The symbolism of the capsule's name in relation to the original Liberty Bell is obvious. When the name was painted on the capsule, a crack, symbolizing the one on the original Liberty Bell, was also added. Grissom later remarked: "Ever since my flight, which ended up with the capsule sinking to the bottom of the Atlantic, there has been a joke around the Cape that that was the last capsule we would ever launch with a crack in it."

The souvenir patch, which commemorates Grissom's flight, is shaped like a bell to underscore the symbolism he chose in naming his capsule. The background and border are grey, forming the bell's shape. A black oval area at the bottom adds a three-dimensional look to the patch, as if the bell were swinging towards us.

On the right side, a black crack-line runs up into the body completing the symbolic rendering. The capsule is outlined in sky blue with black fill and trails six gold mylar lines indicating the flight path. Grissom's name is sewn on the capsule with gold mylar, and the capsule's name, *Liberty Bell 7*, is embroidered at the base, also in gold mylar thread. Mercury 4, the mission designation, is sewn in red, forming an arc above the capsule.

Mercury-Atlas 5 was an unmanned orbital flight launched on November 29, 1961. The capsule was unnamed and the only crew was Enos the chimp. The capsule was recovered after a three-hour, sixteen-minute flight. Enos survived despite having to endure 7.8 gravities during re-entry. He also suffered 79 electric shocks caused by malfunctioning control levers. Enos had been trained to operate the levers in order to avoid shocks. When the malfunction occurred, Enos was continually shocked. In spite of this, he continued to operate the levers. Because this was an unmanned flight, no patch has ever been made to commemorate it.

Mercury-Atlas 6 carried astronaut John Glenn into earth orbit on February 20, 1962. Glenn became the first American astronaut to orbit the earth, and was hailed as a hero upon his return from space. This was the only flight Glenn ever made into space, but it made his name a household word. His flight is still remembered as a milestone in America's space endeavors. Glenn retired from NASA two years after his mission, and in 1974 became the first astronaut to enter politics when he was elected a U.S. Senator from Ohio.

Glenn's flight lasted just under five hours as he orbited the globe three times. A telemetry fault caused grave concern by indicating that the capsule's heat shield was no longer locked in position. It was decided that Glenn not jettison the vehicle's retropack before re-entry in hope that this would help retain the heat shield in its proper position. The heat shield held, and Glenn landed safely in the Atlantic waters off the east coast of Florida.

Glenn chose to name his capsule *Friendship 7* to underscore the importance of space exploration for the entire world. He also wanted to stress how much the earth itself is simply a neighborhood, something all of the astronauts seem to feel after viewing the "Big Blue Marble" from the distant vista of outer space. In Glenn's words: "Flying around the world, over all those countries, that was the message I wanted to convey."

The souvenir patch for Mercury 6 depicts the *Friendship 7* flying over the earth's neighborhoods. The emblem is round, and is 3" in diameter. It has a black overlock border. Centered at the bottom is the earth; the Atlantic waters are sewn in light blue, the Florida peninsula in light green. Three trails of silver mylar thread circle the globe, symbolizing each orbit of the flight. The background of the patch is navy twill, representing deep space. Against this background, above the earth, *Friendship 7* is sewn in white and silver mylar thread. The words are sewn into the shape of a capsule which is beginning its re-entry. At the top, sewn in green, is the mission designation, Mercury 6. At the bottom, Glenn's name is sewn in white thread.

The next flight in the Mercury series was Mercury-Atlas 7. Scott Carpenter was the pilot for this mission, which was launched from Cape Canaveral on May 24, 1962. Carpenter's flight, like Glenn's, lasted just under five hours and made three orbits of the earth. Carpenter's capsule, the *Aurora 7*, overshot the Atlantic landing site by over 250 miles, causing him to float in the sea some three hours before recovery ships could reach him. Carpenter also has the distinction of being the first astronaut to eat in space.

The souvenir patch commemorating Carpenter's flight is a 3" square. The emblem has a maroon border with an orange twill background. At the bottom, a light-blue globe can be seen, with a yellow-gold sun rising over the horizon. The sun splays yellow-gold rays throughout the patch. Above the earth, the *Aurora 7* capsule is depicted in light-blue and yellow-gold hues. Above it, in white, is the mission designation. The name Aurora is embroidered below the capsule in white thread. A large 7, sewn in silver mylar, intersects the capsule name between the A and U. Behind the 7 are three rings, two yellow gold and one white, representing the three orbits of the flight. Carpenter chose the name Aurora for his craft because of its celestial significance and because as a child in Colorado, he lived on the corner of Aurora and 7th Streets.

Mercury-Atlas 8 carried Walter Schirra into orbit on October 3, 1962. Schirra's flight lasted for six orbits and was considered a textbook flight. He was in orbit for just over nine hours, proving that continued efforts in space were justified.

Schirra named his capsule *Sigma 7* to underscore the engineering and technical aspects of space flight. Sigma is a mathematical term meaning "sum of." It is also a letter of the Greek alphabet, represented as a stylized E.

The souvenir patch for Mercury 8 is square, like its predecessor, Mercury 7. The border is a bright red, against a dark navy-blue twill background. The navy color suggests deep space. In the lower right-hand corner, a blue and green earth is orbited by the Greek sigma. An Arabic 7 overlays the sigma. Both are sewn in silver mylar thread and shadowed by light-blue thread. The sigma design trails six lines of silver mylar around the earth, representing the number of orbits in the flight. A large gold 8 can be seen on the left side of the patch, thus designating the mission number. The word Mercury is embroidered in gold inside the upper half of the 8.

The final mission of the Mercury series was Mercury-Atlas 9. Gordon Cooper flew aloft on May 15, 1963 in *Faith 7*. His mission encompassed twenty-two orbits and lasted just over thirty-four hours. Cooper carried out experiments aimed at developing a guidance and navigation system for the Apollo spacecrafts. As always, the real goal of the Space Program, was the landing (and safe return) of men on the moon.

Cooper chose the name *Faith 7* for his capsule because "an awful lot of thought and symbolism had gone into all those earlier names. I felt a certain responsibility. I selected the name *Faith 7* to show my faith in my fellow workers, my faith in all the hardware so carefully tested, my faith in myself and my faith in God. The more you study, the more you know all the scientific stuff, it correlates. It confirms religious faith." The name *Faith 7* was painted on the spacecraft and surrounded by a five-pointed star.

The souvenir patch for Mercury 9 is octagonal in shape. The patch has a deep-red border encompassing a light-blue twill background. In the center is a large 9, sewn in gold, designating the mission. Above it, also sewn in gold, is the name Mercury. The eye of the 9 contains a blue and green earth. The base of the 9 trails gold lines symbolizing the orbital flight path. These reach upwards to a silver and blue capsule, which is embroidered to the left of the 9. On its right, a five-pointed silver mylar star is outlined in blue. Inside the star is the capsule's name, *Faith 7*, embroidered in royal blue.

3 ▪ THE GEMINI PROGRAM

Gemini was the successor to Project Mercury. Gemini spacecraft were twice the weight of the Mercury capsules, and relied heavily on the technology developed during those first six manned flights. At the same time, Gemini craft were more advanced and complex. They bridged the gap between the end of the Mercury Program and the beginnings of Apollo. Gemini provided our space program with invaluable experience in the areas of rendezvous, space docking, long-term flight capability, extra-vehicular activity (EVA), and self-guided re-entry. Gemini established the United States as the firm leader in the race to space and, in particular, to the moon.

The first two flights of the Gemini Program were unmanned hardware tests. Following the precedent of Mercury, no patches were ever commissioned for these missions. The first seven flights in Gemini (including the two unmanned missions) were powered by Titan 2 rockets and were thus code named GT. The final five missions included an Agena rocket being launched into orbit as a docking target. For this reason, these missions carried the designation, GTA.

Gemini became the first flight program to have a program insignia. The program patch is a round, 3" diameter emblem. The background is a disc of dark navy-blue twill, with a matching overlock border. Located in the center of the patch is a gold zodiac Gemini symbol. A white star on each of the two vertical curves of the zodiac symbol represent Pollux and Castor, the Gemini twins of the zodiac. Aptly named, Gemini missions were to always carry two astronauts.

According to Gus Grissom, Alex Nagy of NASA Headquarters was the first to suggest the name, "and it caught on overnight." Coincidentally, Gemini, as a sign of the zodiac, is controlled by Mercury. Thus, the name of our second manned space project seemed to be favorably blessed by the very stars it aimed to lead us towards.

The first manned Gemini mission was Gemini 3. The flight was a short, three-orbit mission, launched in March of 1965. This mission carried the first computer into space, enabling Grissom, the flight commander, to compute the thrust needed to change the spacecraft's orbit. This meant that an astronaut now could totally control his craft in space. No one could ever again say that the astronauts were only along for the ride, as some claimed during the Mercury Program.

Grissom and Young named their spacecraft the *Molly Brown*, a tongue-in-cheek reference to Grissom's Mercury flight. Grissom's Mercury capsule sank in the ocean and was lost, when the hatch blew prematurely as he was waiting for recovery ships to reach him. *Molly Brown* refers to the musical comedy, *The Unsinkable Molly Brown*, which was closing a successful run on Broadway when Gemini 3 was launched skyward.

At this time, NASA had not yet begun to design emblems for each space mission. Like the Mercury Program, the early Gemini mission patches are a result of souvenir collectors' and space enthusiasts' demand for memorabilia. The souvenir patch for Gemini 3 is a 3" diameter, round patch. The background is a dark olive-green twill, surrounded by an orange overlock border. The Gemini capsule is sewn into the center of the patch using white, orange and red thread. Above the capsule, the mission designation, GT-3, is sewn in orange to match the border. The astronauts' names are embroidered in NASA-red, and inscribe an arc at the top of the patch. At the bottom, sewn in white, is the name of that unsinkable craft, the *Molly Brown*.

Gemini 4 lifted off from Cape Kennedy on June 3, 1965 and splashed down four days later in the Atlantic (June 7, 1965). Astronaut Jim McDivitt was forced to make a manual re-entry when the capsule's computer failed. Gemini 4 is particularly remembered as the mission that included the first "space walk" by an American astronaut. For twenty-one minutes, at the end of a tether, Ed White maneuvered about, outside the capsule. He became the first American to leave the relative safety of his capsule and brave the vacuum of space. His movements were powered by a hand-held thruster.

The emblem celebrating Gemini 4 is also a souvenir patch. It is round and 3" in diameter. The background of the emblem is NASA-red twill, and the patch has an aqua-colored overlock border. At the bottom of the patch, the Gemini capsule is embroidered in white. Above it, and attached by a white tether, astronaut Ed White is portrayed making the first EVA (Extra-Vehicular Activity) by an American astronaut. The astronauts' names are also sewn in white; McDivitt's to the left, and White's to the right. The upper half of the patch is embroidered with the mission designation, Gemini 4 in white. Just below it, the phrase First Space Walk is embroidered in light gold.

Gemini 5 was an eight-day mission that proved man could withstand the rigors of space for as long as it would take to fly to the moon, stay a short time and return to earth. Gordon Cooper and Pete Conrad were launched into orbit on August 21, 1965. Their mission kept them orbiting the earth until August 28. Gemini 5 completed 120 orbits of our globe, and was the first extended manned space flight in history. Gemini 5 also had the distinction of providing another first for America's Space Program: this was the first mission to have a specially designed, official crew patch.

On August 14, 1965, NASA Administrator James E. Webb wrote this in a memo to NASA personnel: "On GT-5 and future Gemini flights, such an identification (patch) may be worn on the right breast beneath the nameplate of the Astronaut. . . . For Gemini flights after GT-5, the crew commander or senior pilot will be permitted to designate or design or recommend a patch for his flight, subject to approval by both the Director of the Manned Spacecraft Center and the Associate Administrator for Manned Spaceflight at NASA Headquarters."

Since then, the tradition has been upheld. Since Gemini 5, every manned mission flown by NASA has been identified with an official embroidered emblem. These are worn by the flight crews, NASA ground crews and contractor support personnel. In addition, they are available to the public and to collectors through NASA Exchanges, Base Visitor Centers, science museum and planetarium shops, and other retail commercial sources.

The Gemini 5 patch is a 3" diameter, round patch. The background is white twill, and the patch has a black overlock border. Dominating the center of the patch is a Conestoga wagon, embroidered with a black and silver body. The wagon cover is sewn in white. The phrase 8 Days or Bust is embroidered in red onto the wagon cover. Above the wagon, also in red, is the mission designation. Cooper is sewn in red in the lower left quadrant of the patch, while the lower right quadrant is embroidered with Conrad, also in red. The astronauts' names are joined by a black circle, sewn in a complete circle just inside the border of the emblem. This black circle represents the orbital flight path of Gemini 5.

The "8 Days or Bust" motto was left off the crew's emblems during the flight, and was added only after the successful completion of the mission. This was a result of Administrator Webb's concern that should the flight not go the full eight days "there are many who are going to say it was 'busted.'" Of course, Gemini 5 did go eight days, and all subsequent renderings of the patch do carry the "8 Days or Bust" motto.

The covered wagon was chosen as the symbol of Gemini 5 because Cooper wanted to emphasize the pioneering nature of the early missions of the Space Program. In Cooper's words: ". . . Pete and I tackled them with the idea of a crew patch. My father-in-law had whittled a model of a covered wagon and I thought that was a good way to symbolize the pioneering nature of these early flights. The eight days or bust wording just sort of followed along naturally."

Gemini 7 became the next flight in this program. 7 launched from the Cape on December 4, 1965, carrying Frank Borman and James Lovell into orbit. Gemini 7 was designed to be a long duration flight. Its main objectives were to perform medical experiments, and to further study man's limits of endurance in a deep-space environment. Gemini 7 also became the rendezvous target for Gemini 6 when that mission's Agena target rocket failed to achieve orbit.

Gemini 7's patch is a round, 3″ diameter emblem. It has a dark navy-blue overlock border, surrounding a dark-navy twill background. Lovell and Borman chose a torch to symbolize medicine and endurance in the tradition of a long-distance runner. The symbol is particularly apropos since Gemini 7 was designed especially to be a mission of endurance. It was, for its time, the longest space flight in human experience. The crew's capsule is embroidered in white and is located on the left side of the patch. Dominating the center is a white hand and the torch, capped by a gold flame. A white Roman numeral VII can be seen on the right of the patch, symbol of the mission designation. The astronauts' names are sewn in a white arc above the torch flame. The flame curls back to the left side of the patch, implying motion. This is meant to symbolize the long time span of Gemini 7's mission. Lovell later said that "the artwork was done by NASA artists." Even though this patch is very basic in design and color, it captures the mood of the Gemini program well. The Gemini 7 patch always leaves one with a feeling for the determined, futuristic mind-set of our early space explorers.

Gemini 6 was launched eleven days after Gemini 7, leaving the pad at Cape Kennedy on December 15, 1965. Her crew were Wally Schirra, a veteran of the Mercury 8 mission, and Thomas Stafford, who was embarking on his first journey into outer space. Gemini 6 suffered three delays in her launch schedule before she was finally able to join Gemini 7 in earth orbit. Her original flight plan called for a rendezvous with an unmanned Agena rocket. However, this plan had to be scrapped when the Agena drone failed to achieve orbit and was lost. Gemini 6 joined Gemini 7 in orbit, and they spent nearly a full day in orbit together. Schirra was able to bring the Gemini 6's capsule within 6 feet of Gemini 7, achieving the first rendezvous of two manned craft in space. Gemini 6 returned to earth after this historic event on December 16. She made a mere sixteen orbits of the earth, compared to Gemini 7's two hundred and six. Her elapsed time for the entire mission was twenty-five hours and fifty-one minutes.

The design of the Gemini 6 patch has very special symbolic reference for celestial observers. Schirra wanted the patch design to represent the night sky that would be visible when the rendezvous maneuver took place. In his own words: "I designed the patch to locate in the sixth hour of celestial right ascension. This was the predicted celestial area where the rendezvous should occur (that is, in the constellation Orion). It finally did occur there. The flight patch had an Agena target rather than a Gemini as in real life." To this day, the official patch is produced with an Agena target embroidered in the center of the constellation. The original target was an Agena, and when the drone was lost, and replaced by Gemini 7, it was too late to change the crew's patch.

The Gemini 6 patch is hexagonal in shape, symbolic of the mission designation, as well as the celestial connotation. The background is black twill, to represent deep space. The border is a lemon-yellow color, in an overlock style. The mission designation and the astronauts' names are all embroidered in white. The stars are also sewn in white and surrounded by a lemon-yellow outline. This is meant to represent the twinkling effect produced by the earth's atmosphere when observing the sky from the ground. The Agena is sewn in lemon-yellow, plainly visible in the line of the large 6, which also represents the mission designation.

Gemini VIII carried Neil Armstrong and David Scott into orbit on March 16, 1966. They were to return home nearly eleven hours later in an emergency splashdown off the coast of Florida. This did not happen, however, until the two men had completed the first successful docking maneuver in the history of space flight, linking their craft with an orbiting Agena target rocket. Problems arose when the linked spacecraft began to tumble and spin out of control. This was caused by a jammed thruster on the Gemini capsule. The tumbling made it extremely difficult to disengage, and the crew were very close to passing out when a successful escape was managed by firing the capsule's retro-rockets. Shortly thereafter, they returned to earth, a bit shaken, but safe.

Gemini VIII became America's first space emergency.

Like many of the Gemini patches, the emblem for Gemini VIII is a 3″ diameter, round patch. The background is white twill. The patch is bordered with a light-blue overlock border. The astronauts' names are embroidered in navy thread, one above the other, in the upper left quadrant of the patch. To their right is a prism, splitting the light of Pollux and Castor into a spectrum of light which forms the zodiac symbol for Gemini, followed by a Roman numeral VIII. The VIII is, of course, the numeric designation for this Gemini mission.

The objectives of Gemini VIII were meant to encompass the objectives of the entire Gemini Program, that is, EVA, experiments, rendezvous, and docking. The spectrum of light created by the prism symbolizes the notion that the flight objectives covered the complete spectrum of the Gemini Program's objectives.

Gemini 9 is also known as the unlucky flight. Elliot See and Charles Bassett II were named as the original crew for this mission. They were killed in a plane crash in St. Louis as they attempted to land their jet in bad weather. In a grimly ironic circumstance, their plane crashed at the McDonnell plant, striking the factory roof only yards from where their capsule was being assembled. The backup crew, Thomas Stafford and Eugene Cernan, were named to fly the mission in their place. Stafford and Cernan endured two delays in the launch before they were finally able to lift off on June 3, 1966. Once in orbit, the mission suffered more bad luck. The fiberglass cover on the target Agena failed to open, thus preventing the Gemini capsule from docking. Cernan did perform a two-hour spacewalk, and there was speculation that he might attempt to remove the Agena's shield manually. The idea was dropped, however, as being too dangerous, and the spacecraft returned to earth without linking up to the crippled target.

The patch design for Gemini IX is unique. Unlike most of its predecessors, the Gemini IX patch forsakes a circular design, opting instead for that of a shield. The patch has a deep navy-blue twill background. The border is Irregulier (this allows the patch to "blend into" the material to which it is applied, making it look more like a part of the overall fabric) and is oversewn in silver thread.

The center of the patch contains a large, white, Roman numeral IX, the mission designation. Superimposed on the IX are a light-blue Gemini capsule and a similarly colored Agena. They are positioned to show the typical Gemini-Agena docking profile. A silver astronaut can be seen just below the Agena, tethered by a silver line to the Gemini capsule. His tether forms an Arabic 9, another symbolic reference to the mission designation. The astronauts' names are sewn in light blue below the spacecraft configurations.

Gemini X was a three-day mission, launched from Cape Kennedy on July 18, 1966 and returning to earth on July 21. Her crew were astronauts John Young and Michael Collins. Gemini X was a highly successful flight in the Gemini series, and achieved several notable accomplishments. First, Young and Collins maneuvered their capsule into a perfect docking with an Agena target. Using the Agena's rockets, they then boosted their capsule to a new orbital altitude record. Once in her new orbit, Gemini X separated from the Agena and rendezvoused with Gemini 8's Agena target, which had been left in a parking orbit for just such a purpose. Mike Collins then spacewalked over to the waiting Agena, retrieving scientific equipment, which was returned to earth.

The emblem for Gemini X reverts to the round shape that marks most of the emblems in the Gemini series. It has a 3″ diameter, with a medium-blue twill background. The border is a navy color, in overlock style. A large red Roman numeral is embroidered in the center of the patch. It is, of course, the symbol of the mission designation. Two spacecraft, a Gemini capsule and an Agena target drone, orbit the numeral in a chase pattern prior to rendezvous. The twin stars of Gemini are sewn onto the Roman numeral in yellow thread. At the top, Young is embroidered in navy thread. Collins is sewn in the same color at the bottom of the patch. The chase sequence of the Gemini capsule and the Agena target is the major important symbol of the Gemini X patch. It represents the most important objective of the mission, which was the twin rendezvous with the two targets.

Gemini XI lifted off from Cape Kennedy on September 12, 1966. The mission would last until September 15. Gemini XI smashed the altitude record set by Gemini X when Pete Conrad and Richard Gordon, Jr., flew her and her Agena target to an altitude of eight hundred fifty miles. The astronauts' rendezvous with their target was successful. This was an important event, since such maneuvering abilities would be necessary for any successful attempts to visit the moon. Later, Gordon connected the two craft with a tether line during one of two spacewalks he would make during the flight. When the two craft were undocked, the Gemini's thrusters were fired, causing the two craft to move in a cartwheel motion. This produced .00015g, an event marking the first attempt to create artificial gravity in space. Gemini XI also became the first mission to allow the computer to fly the spacecraft all the way home through re-entry. This was an important event, since automatic, computer-controlled re-entry would be a necessity on the moon flights.

The Gemini XI patch is another which departs from the more familiar round shape of most Gemini emblems. The overall shape of the patch is meant to represent the shape of the Gemini capsule. The patch has a navy-blue twill background and a gold overlock border. Conrad and Gordon were both Navy fliers, and chose to emphasize navy blue and gold throughout the emblem motif since they are the Navy colors. Four white stars can be seen located throughout the patch. Each symbolizes a particular event of Gemini XI's mission: The first, closest to earth, symbolizes the first orbit rendezvous with the target vehicle. The second, located near the docked Gemini and Agena spacecraft, is symbolic of that event. Gordon's spacewalk is marked by another star embroidered just below the tethered astronaut on the right of the patch. At the top, a fourth star represents the eight-hundred-fifty-mile orbital record achieved by the two spacecraft. The Roman numeral XI can be seen rising from the earth, symbolic of the mission designation and also of the new altitude record.

Gemini XII, the last mission of the Gemini series, rocketed into space on November 11, 1966 and returned five days later on November 15. The crew were Jim Lovell and Edwin (Buzz) Aldrin, Jr. Aldrin was to perform three separate spacewalks on this mission, totaling over five and one-half hours. These were the most successful and longest duration EVA's up to this point.

Gemini XII also rendezvoused and docked with an Agena target three times, performing artificial-gravity experiments. The spacecraft made a fully automatic re-entry with computer guidance, ending one of the most trouble-free missions in the highly successful Gemini series.

Gemini XII was originally scheduled to fly on or about Halloween. For this reason, Lovell and Aldrin emphasized Halloween colors in their mission patch. The gold space capsule is outlined in orange, and the Roman numeral XII is sewn completely in orange thread. The background of the patch is black twill, another Halloween color also symbolic of deep space. The emblem is a round, 3" diameter size, as were most Gemini patches. The patch border is a black, overlock style. The spacecraft also acts as a clock hand, pointing directly at the Roman numeral twelve, Halloween's symbolic "witching hour." A golden crescent moon is depicted in the left half of the patch. Lovell and Aldrin chose the moon not only for its associations with Halloween but also because the final Gemini flight pointed to the upcoming Apollo moon missions. Lovell credited artists at McDonnell Douglas with the design renderings of the patch.

4 ▪ THE APOLLO PROGRAM

The Apollo Program has become, for many Americans, the high-water mark of the American Space Program. Even the splendor and excitement of the Space Shuttle has not captured the imagination and spirit of the American public in the way Apollo did. There was something magical and special about those days when we raced to be the first men on the moon. Americans were to truly become the first interplanetary travellers in earth's history. Science fiction was rapidly becoming science fact; and, as our successes grew, many of us dreamed of colonies in space and brave new worlds waiting to be explored. Books, movies and even television shows urged us all to "boldly go where no man has gone before."

Apollo became more than just an American dream. Television brought coverage of NASA's ambitious undertaking to all the people of the world. The earth's inhabitants waited expectantly for each launch, and marvelled at the immensity of the task. To leave the bonds of earth and travel to her moon was the boldest undertaking of this generation. Man learned to fly early in the century. Now, near its end, he was reaching beyond boundaries that had seemed impassable. Apollo's three-man spacecraft was first proposed by NASA in July of 1960. The spaceship would be designed for earth orbital and circumlunar flights, and would be launched by a Saturn-1 type rocket.

In May of 1961, President Kennedy proposed that the United States establish as a national goal a manned landing on the moon by the end of the decade. He outlined the goals of America's Space Program in an address to Congress: "Now is the time . . . for this nation to take a clearly leading role in space achievement, which in many ways may hold the key to our future on earth. . . . this is not merely a race. We go into space because whatever mankind must undertake, free men must fully share."

The space race had begun with the Russian Sputnik on October 4, 1957. The United States had now accepted the challenge and named the prize: All glory and honor to the first men on the moon. When President Kennedy spoke those words to Congress on May 25, 1961, Alan Shepard was the *only* American to have flown in outer space. But the Apollo Program was to bear the fruit of Kennedy's words. Apollo would prove, convincingly, that man could leave his earthly home and travel to the stars.

Plans for a manned lunar mission were actually begun in April of 1957. In July of 1960, NASA formally named the Lunar Project Apollo, and established five main goals:

1. To land American astronauts on the moon and return them safely to earth.

2. To generate the technology and hardware needed to meet other national interests in space.

3. To make America the clear-cut leader in the race to space.

4. To carry out a program of scientific exploration of the moon.

5. To develop and enhance man's ability to work in space and lunar environments.

The program patch for the Apollo missions is usually called the Apollo A, due to the large stylized A which can be seen in the center of the patch. It is normally found in several sizes. The official patch is made in a 3" and an 8" diameter. Both are beautifully embroidered and are made with an overlock border to match the grey background of the outer circle. This color is meant to represent moondust. A souvenir version exists in a 2" diameter. It follows the design of the official patch closely, but black outlines around Orion's Belt are left out. Also, the detail of color in the moon and the earth are not as striking.

The background of the emblem depicts the constellation Orion, positioned so that its three central stars (Orion's belt) form the bar of the A. These stars are Mintaka, Alnilam, and Alnitak. Above the moon is another star, the red giant, Betelgeuse, which forms Orion's shoulder. His opposite shoulder is the white star, Bellatrix, which is seen on the right top side of the A. Under the left leg of the A is Saiph, a blue-white star. It forms one of Orion's feet. The other foot is formed by the blue-white star Rigel, which is located under the right leg of the A. Rigel was also one of the navigational stars used by the astronauts of Apollo.

The face of the moon represents the mythical god Apollo. Finally, a double trajectory passes behind the moon, the earth, and the central stars of the emblem. This signifies the voyage out and back, from earth to the moon. Apollo was the god of the sun in Greek mythology. Choosing his name for man's greatest journey into outer space was indeed fitting. Apollo pulled the sun across the sky each day, riding in his horse-drawn chariot. The astronauts of Apollo flew their "chariots" farther into space than man had ever been, pulling his hopes and dreams across the heavens.

The first Apollo Command Module was placed into orbit by a Saturn I rocket on May 28, 1964. Continued development of the spacecraft and the Saturn rocket were proceeding well until the events of January 27, 1967. Apollo 1, the first manned Apollo flight, was being ground-tested on launch pad #34 at Cape Kennedy. The astronauts, Ed White, Gus Grissom and Roger Chaffee, were running a "plugs out" test, making sure that the lunar ship could sustain itself without ground power. They had climbed into the capsule at about 1:00 P.M., and were sealed inside to run a simulation of the actual countdown, which was scheduled to take place some three weeks later. Pure oxygen was pumped into the cabin. The tests proceeded normally during the afternoon with the exception of radio communications between the crew and ground control. Grissom's increasing irritation with this problem was evident when he remarked, "How are we going to get to the moon, when we can't even talk between three towers?"

The tests continued until, at 6:31 P.M., a cry came over the radio from inside the capsule: "There is a fire in here." An electrical arc from wiring inside the capsule had started a fire which doomed the three astronauts inside. It took several minutes to open the capsule, and by the time ground personnel reached them it was too late—the astronauts were dead.

They had been asphyxiated by toxic fumes. Their deaths delayed the launch of the first manned Apollo for eighteen months. Apollo 1 never flew. In memory of her crew, their patch was later carried to the moon's surface by the crew of Apollo 11.

Apollo 1 is one of the few emblems made for a manned mission that never flew. The official version is 4" in diameter, and is a fully embroidered patch. The center of the patch depicts the Apollo Command Module orbiting the earth. As is often true of NASA patches, the Florida peninsula can be seen below the module. The land masses are sewn in light-tan thread, while the oceans are sewn in light blue. The Command Module is embroidered in white and outlined in black. In the distance, just clearing the earth's horizon, the moon is visible. It, too, is sewn in white thread, and ringed with silver mylar, which creates a soft halo effect.

Surrounding the space scene, a yellow-gold band forms a circle on the interior of the patch. The astronauts' names, White, Grissom, and Chaffee are sewn in black thread in the upper half of the circle. The mission designation, Apollo 1, appears in the lower half, and is also sewn in black thread. Finally, the outer area of the patch provides a background of the American flag, embroidered in red, white, and blue. The border of the patch is black, sewn in an overlock style.

A 3" souvenir version of the patch follows primarily the same design. However, the gold band is twill background material, not embroidery. In addition, the earth is sewn with gold and navy blue thread. This differs dramatically from the official version. One other design difference can be noted in the moon. It is sewn as a crescent, in the same gold thread which forms the earth's land masses. Like the official version, the souvenir emblem does have a black overlock border as a sign of mourning for the lost crew.

On November 9, 1967, the Apollo Program began to move forward from the tragedy of Apollo 1 with the launch of an unmanned Command Module on a Saturn 5 rocket. The module was successfully placed into orbit. This launch was designated Apollo 4 and had no patch. Apollo 5 launched in January of 1968, again as an unmanned mission. Mission 5 was a successful test of the Lunar Module systems. This included firing both the ascent and descent propulsion systems while parked in earth orbit. Since it was an unmanned mission, Apollo 5 also had no mission patch.

Apollo 6 provided the second unmanned test of the combined Apollo Command Module on a Saturn 5. It was launched from Cape Kennedy in April of 1968. The rocket experienced problems in the first stage with "pogo" vertical oscillations, but the Apollo hardware performed very well.

Pogo oscillations are caused by short-term variations in rocket thrust. As a result of these oscillations, an astronaut would experience very uncomfortable axial accelerations. Also, in a large rocket like the Saturn 5, "pogos" could result in severe propellant sloshing. This sloshing could cause the rocket to abort or explode. Obviously, this was not a minor problem. However, feeling that the problem was solvable, plans proceeded for the launch of Apollo 7, the first manned Apollo spaceshot.

Apollo 7 carried both the Command and Service Modules of the Apollo hardware, but did not carry a Lunar Module. The mission lifted off from Cape Kennedy on October 11, 1968, carrying astronauts Walter Schirra, Donn Eisele and Walter Cunningham. The mission lasted for almost eleven days and provided a highly successful test of the operational qualities of the Apollo hardware.

Apollo 7 set a pattern of success which was to carry through the entire program. Apollo 7 also provides an interesting historical footnote: This mission broadcast the first live television transmissions from a manned spacecraft. In addition, the astronauts of Apollo 7 spent more man hours in space than had been spent on all the Soviet space flights combined, up to that time.

The official patch for Apollo 7 is a 4" diameter emblem. An elliptical orbital trail in the upper half of the patch extends just enough so that the emblem is not perfectly round. It is a fully embroidered emblem, with a black, overlock border. The background is dark navy-blue thread, symbolizing the depth of space. The earth is centered in the patch, depicting the North and South American continents. They are sewn in light green against light blue oceans. Near the top of the globe, in the foreground, the Apollo capsule and Service Module are sewn in white with black detail. The spacecraft trails an ellipse of orange flame around the globe, symbolizing the earth orbital nature of the flight. The crew's names are embroidered in an arc at the bottom of the patch; and are sewn in white thread. A Roman numeral VII is sewn in the Pacific region of the globe. It is, of course, the mission designation. The numeral is sewn in orange thread and outlined in black.

Walt Cunningham describes the patch: "It was our original intention to emphasize the first manned Apollo (Apollo 1) and the recovery from the fire on the pad aspects as well. We considered depicting a spacecraft rising from a ball of fire and calling it the Phoenix. The patch designed was subject to NASA approval and we abandoned the Phoenix theme, feeling it would be rejected as in bad taste. I zeroed in on a circle (for the earth), and an ellipse (for orbit). The orbital plane was tilted for artistic reasons."

A 3" souvenir version of the emblem is also available. It duplicates the official patch remarkably well. Other than the difference in size, there is only one other major difference. The 3" version has a navy twill background instead of an embroidered one. The color match is quite good, however, and it is an attractive addition to any collection of space patches.

Apollo 8 was the second manned Apollo flight. It launched from Cape Kennedy on December 21, 1968, and returned to earth on December 27. Her crew included Frank Borman (Commander), Jim Lovell (Command Pilot), and Bill Anders (Lunar Module Pilot).

This was the first mission to be launched by the huge Saturn 5 rocket. It was also the first manned space flight to journey to earth's moon. Apollo 8 orbited the moon ten times, obtaining film and photographs of the moon's surface, including the far side, which had never before been seen by human eyes. It was during this flight that

Frank Borman took the now famous "earthrise" photograph, which captures the earth rising above the moon's horizon. Borman also touched the heart of the entire world with his readings from Genesis on Christmas morning, as Apollo orbited the moon. The mission was so perfect that splashdown in the Pacific ended Apollo 8's journey only eleven seconds earlier than the time in the flight plan. That time had been computed many months beforehand.

The Apollo 8 patch is unique. Its shape is designed to represent the Apollo capsule. In the official version, it is a 4" emblem. The patch is fully embroidered with a deep royal-blue background. This symbolizes, as it has before, the color of deep space. The entire patch is sewn with a white overlock border. A red figure 8 represents both Apollo 8 and the flight path of the spacecraft on its journey to the moon and back. The figure 8 is outlined in black, and the astronauts' names are sewn on its bottom with white thread. Inside the lower half of the figure, the earth is sewn in light blue, tan, and dark brown. Continents, and the globe itself, are outlined in black. The North American continent is the most visible and identifiable land mass. The moon is located in the upper half of the figure 8, and is sewn in tan and ecru. It, too, is outlined in black thread.

The most common souvenir version of the patch is sewn in a 3" size. It differs from the official in that it has a black border and a navy-blue twill background. The figure 8 is sewn in orange, rather than red, and is not outlined.

The Apollo 8 astronauts wanted to name their spacecraft, but NASA disagreed and the idea was forgotten. They had chosen the name *Columbiad* after the cannon in Jules Verne's novel, *From the Earth to the Moon*, because there were many similarities between their flight and that of Verne's fictional account of a voyage to the moon, which was written nearly one hundred years before the launch of Apollo 8. The similarities to Verne's book provide several interesting (and perhaps eerie) coincidences.

Apollo 8 and *Columbiad* both carried three astronauts. Apollo 8's crew were Borman, Lovell and Anders. Verne's rocket carried Barbicane, Nicholl and Ardan. Note the similarities in name between Borman and Barbicane, and Anders and Ardan. Say the names aloud to appreciate their similarity. Nicholl and Lovell end with a similar sound, but these names have another interesting connection, as well. Michael Collins was originally to have flown on Apollo 8, but surgery on a bone spur on his spine caused him to step aside for his backup, Jim Lovell. Compare the sound of Collins and Nicholl as you say them aloud. Again, the similarity is interesting.

In addition to similar name sounds, the two space missions had other circumstances in common. Both Apollo 8 and *Columbiad* were launched in December. Also, both missions were launched from Florida. Apollo 8 was, of course, launched from Cape Kennedy. According to Verne's book, Columbiad launched from a site roughly one hundred miles west of the Cape.

Apollo 9 was the first manned Apollo flight to carry the Lunar Module. It was launched into orbit on March 3, 1969. This mission was confined to earth orbit in order to test the LEM and other equipment. The LEM separated from the Command Module, then rendezvoused and docked again.

This operation was carried out under conditions simulating those the astronauts would face on actual moon-landing missions. On the fourth day of the mission Commander James McDivitt and LEM Pilot Russell Schweickhart entered the Lunar Module and separated from the Command Module. Command Module Pilot David Scott remained aboard. The two craft drew apart to a distance of approximately one hundred fifteen miles. The LEM then jettisoned its descent stage and fired the ascent stage, simulating lift-off from the moon. The two craft successfully rendezvoused and docked, returning to earth on March 13. The tests performed by Apollo 9 were of major importance to the continuance of the Apollo program. It would now be only about four months until man took his first steps on another world.

The official Apollo 9 patch is a 4" diameter, round emblem. It has a red overlock border, surrounding a fully embroidered background of royal blue. Apollo IX is embroidered in white at the bottom of the patch. The astronauts' names are also sewn in white, forming an arc across the top of the patch. In the center of the patch the LEM and the Command Module are depicted in a near-docking view. Nearby stands a Saturn rocket, ready to launch. Each Apollo mission had a number, but NASA gave each flight an alphabetical designation as well. Missions were labelled *A*, *B*, *C* and so on. Apollo 9 was labelled as mission *D* in the sequence. This is noted in the patch by embroidering the interior of the *D* in McDivitt with red thread.

The souvenir version of Apollo 9 follows the official design quite closely, with only minor changes. First, as is common, the souvenir version is only 3″ in diameter. In addition, the background is twill, and of a navy color darker than the official version. The spacecraft, names and mission designations are represented as they are in the official patch.

Apollo 10 lifted off from the Cape on May 18, 1969. Tom Stafford was the Commander, John Young was the Command Pilot, and Eugene Cernan was the Lunar Module Pilot. This mission was the final test—the dress rehearsal—for the first actual moon landing. Apollo 10 would follow very closely the flight plan for Apollo 11. The only major difference would be that Apollo 10's LEM, *Snoopy*, would only simulate a landing, coming within 50,000 feet of the surface of the moon. Meanwhile, *Charlie Brown*, the Command Module, would remain in orbit awaiting its safe return. Had circumstance and desire required it, Apollo 10 could have been the first landing. The LEM rejoined the Command Module after nearly eight hours of free flight and thirty-one orbits of the moon. The rehearsal ended in the morning hours of May 26, leaving all mankind certain that the next one would be the Real Thing!

Apollo 10 achieved several "firsts" while performing its duties in space. The first of these was, of course, the "dress rehearsal" itself. This mission was also the first in the series to use the Lunar Module in lunar orbit. Perhaps the most interesting first for Apollo 10 was its broadcasts of color television from lunar orbit. Black and white television broadcasts from space had become commonplace since the Gemini program. But color television was the closest thing to actually being there.

Now there was no hesitation, no regret. The sorrow of Apollo 1 had begun to fade with the stunning successes of the Apollo missions. Incredibly complex theoretical and physical problems had been overcome. Now we were ready to land on the moon! As spring of 1969 gave way to summer, the entire world focused its attention on the humid marshlands of Cape Kennedy. Here spacemen vied with alligators and egrets for territory and habitat. Here, man would soon begin his most exciting journey. The mighty Saturn looked skyward, poised for "a giant leap for mankind!" No one would be disappointed. The drama would soon begin.

The official design of the Apollo 10 patch is a fully embroidered shield. It has a yellow-gold, overlock border. The background is a light-blue embroidery, surrounding an inner shield of black. At the top, Apollo is sewn in black. The astronauts' names are sewn in silver, forming an inverted horseshoe at the outer edges of the patch. Inside the inner shield, a blue and green moon supports a massive Roman numeral *X*. The Command Module, sewn in white with black trim, flies through the upper *v* of the *X*. Blasting up from near the moon's surface is the Lunar Module. Like the Command Module, it is sewn in white with black trim, and trails rocket-fire of red and yellow.

The patch is concerned with the mechanics and objectives of the mission. The Command Module is in lunar orbit, preparing to dock with the LEM. The large Roman *X* suggests the three-dimensional aspect of sitting on the moon's surface. This helps to underscore the notion that Apollo X could have been the first lunar landing. Its massive size is meant to suggest that Apollo 10 left a permanent impression on the moon, even though *Snoopy* and her crew never actually touched the lunar surface.

The souvenir version of Apollo 10 duplicates the shield design in a 3″ size. The border is of the same type, but the background of the patch is a light-blue twill. Thread colors in the moon's surface are of a lighter green than in the official version, and there are fewer craters on the moon's surface. An aqua blue and light yellow shade the *X* for dimensional effect in the souvenir version. The same effect is created with silver and grey thread in the official patch.

July 16, 1969. Wednesday. Over a million people line the causeway at Cape Kennedy. The streets of Titusville and Cocoa Beach are jammed. Millions more watch their television screens as first, smoke and flame, then the roar, tell them all that Apollo 11 is on its way. Every eye turns skyward, following the trail of the mighty Saturn as it blazes through Florida's morning sky. Launch is achieved with no technical problems, and Apollo

11 is soon on a flight path to the moon. On Sunday, July 20, Neil Armstrong and Buzz Aldrin separate the Lunar Module *Eagle* from the Command Module (named the *Columbia*), fire her descent engine, and begin final approach to the moon's surface. As the craft nears the moon's surface, Armstrong takes manual control of the *Eagle* because the spacecraft is nearing an area littered with rock and boulders. The landing site is located in an area of the moon called the Sea of Tranquillity.

The landing was nearly aborted. Continual malfunction alarms were being called out by Aldrin, and were confirmed by Capcom (Capsule Command or Mission Control). They indicated that one of the LEM's computers was overloading. This computer controlled an important radar system which monitored the LEM's altitude and rate of descent. A descent made too quickly could cause the Lunar Module to impact the moon's surface at a high rate of speed. This would be fatal to the astronauts on board. If the descent was too slow, the LEM might run out of fuel, which would also result in a fatal crash on the lunar surface.

Back on earth, an engineer at Mission Control, Steve Bales, was monitoring the performance of the *Eagle*'s computers. It was his responsibility to decide if the computer would clear itself, making the landing safe; or if it would be necessary to abort. A very quiet Mission Control listened as he softly said "Go, Flight," giving the approval for *Eagle* to continue the landing. Her altitude at the time was approximately 6500 feet above the lunar surface. Bales was later awarded the Medal of Freedom (America's highest civilian honor) for his calm, cool judgment.

It was now 4:17 P.M. EDT on Sunday, July 20, 1969. Neil Armstrong's voice echoed throughout Mission Control and all over the world: "Contact light, OK, engine stop. . . . Houston, Tranquillity Base here. The *Eagle* has landed."

The reply from Mission Control was immediate: "Roger, *Tranquillity*. We copy you on the ground. You've got a bunch of guys about to turn blue. We're breathing again. Thanks a lot."

The entire world began to celebrate. Man had finally reached another world, making all things now seem possible. The *Eagle* had reached the lunar surface with less than 2% (30 seconds) of her descent propellant remaining. Apollo 11's flight plan now called for Armstrong and Aldrin to take a rest period of several hours. They decided to forego this, and began to make the preparations for the first lunar EVA. It took some time to don their spacesuits and depressurize *Eagle*, but at last, Armstrong backed out of the spacecraft and descended the ladder attached to the landing leg.

Neil Armstrong became the first man to step on the moon's surface at 10:56 P.M. EDT on Sunday, July 20, 1969. As his left foot touched the grey surface, the entire world heard him say, in words that will never be forgotten: "That's one small step for a man; one giant leap for mankind."

Buzz Aldrin joined him some eighteen minutes later, and the astronauts practiced walking, running, and jumping in the light lunar gravity. They planted an American flag, and received a congratulatory telephone call from President Nixon.

Shortly afterwards, they unveiled a plaque which was left on the moon's surface. It read: "Here men from the planet Earth first set foot upon the Moon, July 1969 A.D. We came in peace for all mankind." It was signed by President Nixon and the three Apollo 11 astronauts. After collecting soil and rock samples, setting up several scientific experiments, and a seismometer (this measured moonquakes and meteorite impacts), the astronauts prepared to rejoin *Columbia*.

Eagle's ascent into lunar orbit, and docking with *Columbia* were successful. The return trip to earth was uneventful, and splashdown on earth occurred at 12:50 P.M. EDT on Thursday, July 24, in the Pacific Ocean southwest of Hawaii. The astronauts were kept in isolation for twenty-one days after leaving the moon's surface to make sure that no lunar contamination was brought back to earth. The Apollo 11 mission lasted eight days, and in that time the astronauts had traveled over 950,000 miles in their journey from earth to the moon, and back.

The official mission patch for Apollo 11 is round, with a 4" diameter. The border of the patch is sewn in overlock style with gold mylar thread. The interior is fully embroidered. A thin, light-blue circle is sewn just inside the border for aesthetic effect. The upper two-thirds (approximately) of the emblem background is sewn in navy thread to symbolize the backdrop of deep space. This area is sewn entirely with horizontal stitching so that it reflects light evenly. This adds to the illusion of depth and dimension. At the top, forming an arc, Apollo 11 is sewn in gold mylar.

The lower third (approximately) of the patch has a white background which delineates the lunar surface. The white thread is sewn over the navy background (which is not visible) with vertical stitching. This adds to the impression that the moon is closer to the viewer, in the foreground of the patch. Detail is added to the moon's surface by sewing craters and other impressions with black and light-blue thread. These stitches are vertical where they "climb" up or down the sides of a crater. They are horizontal where they form flat surfaces.

Poised above the surface of the moon is an American bald eagle. This majestic bird is at once symbolic of the American spirit, and the chosen name of the Lunar Module, *Eagle*. The eagle's wings and claws are extended, in preparation for landing. The torso is sewn with brown and gold thread. The claws and legs are also sewn in gold. The wings are embroidered with a lighter shade of brown; their upper edges and tips lightly touched with gold. The eye and beak are also sewn in gold thread. The head is, of course, sewn with white thread. White can also be seen in the tail. Interestingly, the tail is also sewn with light-blue thread, as well. Detail is added throughout the entire body with black outline.

In its original design, the patch depicted the eagle with an olive branch in his beak, and his claws empty, extended for landing. NASA officials felt that this concept was too aggressive and hostile, so the design was not approved. When the astronauts decided to transfer the branch to the eagle's claws, everyone agreed that the bird's fierce appearance had been softened considerably, and the design was approved. The main stem of the branch is sewn in black thread, its leaves in olive green.

Above, and slightly to the left, of the eagle's head, a small earth can be seen in the background. The left half is sewn in the same navy thread that forms the background of the patch. The stitching is vertical, in an additional layer, so that edges of the planet are distinct and three-dimensional, even though the coloring is identical. The right half of the globe is sewn with light-blue oceans, gold continents (unidentifiable), and white cloud formations.

Amateur astronomers may note that the earth is depicted incorrectly in the official patch. When the earth is viewed from the moon's surface, its shadow would form a crescent at the bottom of the globe. The patch places this shadow at the left side of the earth, in a vertical, rather than horizontal plane. None of the astronauts, NASA officials, or artists at the emblem manufacturer caught this error until after the patch was produced. It was decided to ignore the error, and leave the patch as it was. To this day, the official Apollo 11 patch (and all known souvenir versions) carries this "astronomical glitch."

The most common souvenir version of Apollo 11's patch follows the official one fairly closely. It is smaller, having a diameter of 3". Its border is a yellow-gold overlock rather than gold mylar. The official patch is fully embroidered, while the souvenir version has a navy twill background. There are also some color variations in the eagle. For example, he has no blue in his tail, and no light-gold or dark-brown highlights in his body or wings. In addition, the wings have much less detail than the official version. The earth is sewn with only two thread colors, not three, as in the 4". In spite of the number of differences, the appearance of the souvenir patch is quite good. It is an excellent companion to the official emblem in terms of beauty, clarity, craftsmanship, overall quality and adherence to design. It is highly recommended to any collector of space emblems as a worthy addition to his or her collection.

Apollo 11 inspired several very striking commemorative emblems that also deserve to be included in any complete collection of space emblems. While these are not, strictly speaking, official emblems, they are held in high regard by NASA personnel, and are highly collected. The first of these is a 3" diameter, round patch, called the "Apollo Moonscape." The patch depicts exactly what its name implies—a landscape portrait of the lunar surface.

The patch has a black overlock border, and is fully embroidered. Across the center of the patch is the word Apollo, in deference to the lunar space missions. It is sewn in white thread and outlined in black. To the left center are three white stars, also outlined in black, which form a slight crescent shape in a vertical plane. These stars remind us that three crew members flew on every Apollo mission. The lunar surface is sewn in shades of brown, tan, yellow, and white. Although these colors are not the actual shades of lunar soil, they are certainly more appealing than subtle shades of grey. Details on the moon's surface, such as craters and boulders, are sewn in brown threads, against the multi-colored background.

A 3" patch to commemorate the spacecraft of Apollo 11 is also of interest. It is most commonly called the *Apollo 11, Lem 5*. The name is derived from the number of flights flown by each vehicle. The first moon landing was flown using the eleventh Apollo spacecraft and the fifth Lunar Module in the hardware series.

This patch is round, and has a white twill background. The border is sewn in light-gold overlock style. The lunar surface, at the bottom of the patch, is sewn with silver thread. Surface details are sewn in royal blue. Sitting on the surface of the moon is the Lunar Module. Above it, the Apollo capsule can be seen as it flies by in lunar orbit. In the background, a distant earth appears just above the horizon. All of these objects are embroidered with blue thread.

The basic design of the emblem is a take-off from the official Apollo 11 patch design. The LEM itself replaces the eagle of the original design. The earth is in roughly the same position as in the original. Sewn in red across the top of the patch is the name, *Apollo 11 LEM 5*. The mission patch carries its name in a similar manner. At the bottom, also in red, is the year, 1969, in remembrance of the event.

Two other patches that commemorate Apollo 11 have the same name. They are called the First Lunar Landing emblems. They do differ slightly, but their designs are very similar. The first is a round, 3" diameter patch. It has an overlock border sewn in yellow gold. The background is a deep navy-blue twill, representing deep space. In the foreground, the lunar surface appears, much as it does in the official mission patch. The thread used for the lunar surface is a shade of green that tends toward grey tones. Craters are sewn in white and grey to add detail. The Lunar Module rests on the moon's surface. It is sewn in white, with black thread adding detail. In orbit above can be seen the Apollo capsule; and to the left, the earth rises above the horizon. Like others before it, this emblem borrows much from the official mission emblem.

One interesting feature of the First Lunar Landing patches is that they are the only emblems for Apollo 11 that depict an astronaut. In the 3" version, he is standing on the moon's surface just to the right of the LEM, holding an American flag. You will recall that one of Armstrong and Aldrin's first activities was to erect a flag at their landing site. The words First Lunar Landing 1969 are sewn in white at the top of the patch. At the bottom, USA is sewn in royal blue.

The 4" First Lunar Landing depicts the same scene as the 3" version. It does, however, add more detail. The moon's surface is more clearly defined, showing craters, rocks, hills and mountains. The LEM dominates the center of the patch and is sewn in white with black detail, as in the 3". Above, the Apollo capsule orbits and the earth rises into the lunar sky. First Lunar Landing of Mankind is embroidered in an arc across the top of the patch. It is sewn with white thread. At the bottom, in royal-blue thread, are the words United States of America. In this version, the astronaut stands to the left of the LEM, again holding the American flag. The year 1969 is embroidered to the right of the LEM, and is underlined in red. The background of the 4" First Lunar Landing is navy twill. Its border is overlock style and is sewn in gold mylar.

Apollo 12 left the launch pad at Cape Kennedy on November 14, 1969. It was, of course, our second lunar landing mission. The crew included Commander Pete Conrad, Command Pilot Dick Gordon, and Lunar Module Pilot Al Bean. The Command Module was named *Yankee Clipper*, and the Lunar Module was the *Intrepid*.

From its first moments of flight, Apollo 12 provided much excitement. On launch day, the weather at Cape Kennedy was stormy and raining. There was some question as to whether 12 would even be able to be launched. As the countdown progressed, a small break appeared in the storm, and it was decided to go for launch.

As the Saturn 5 rose skyward through a rain squall, it was struck by lightning. This caused a brief malfunction of the spacecraft's electrical system, and marked the first time that NASA had to consider a launch abort during a manned mission. Apollo 12 did make earth orbit and the electrical problem was solved. This meant that the mission could be cleared for the journey to the moon.

Apollo 12 landed on the moon very near *Surveyor 3*, an early, unmanned lunar probe. In fact, during one of two EVA's, Conrad and Bean visited the *Surveyor*, and recovered its TV camera and other pieces from the *Surveyor*. These items were brought back to earth for further study. In addition, the two astronauts collected rock and soil samples and deployed the first Apollo Lunar Surface Experiment Package (ALSEP).

This contained six scientific experiments which were powered by a nuclear battery (giving it an operational life of at least a year) so that scientists on earth could continue their lunar studies long after Apollo 12 had returned home. The mission concluded safely with splashdown on November 24.

The official patch for the Apollo 12 mission is a round, 4" diameter emblem. Like most of the official patches, it is fully embroidered. The basic color scheme of Apollo 12 is blue and gold. These colors were selected because they are Navy colors, and all three crew members on this mission were Navy people. That is also why the Command Module was nicknamed the *Yankee Clipper*, and the Lunar Module, the *Intrepid*.

The patch is sewn with an overlock style border in royal blue. Just inside this border is a band of white, followed by a wide band of gold mylar. The astronauts' names are embroidered in royal blue in the lower area of the gold mylar band. At the top, Apollo XII is sewn in the same shade of blue. The center of the patch depicts a space scene symbolic of the mission's goals. A Yankee Clipper is seen orbiting the moon's surface. The sailing ship is, of course, symbolic of the Command Module. It carries an American flag at the top of the foremast. The astronauts felt that *Yankee Clipper* embodied the spirit of America, and the spirit of naval camaraderie, as well. The Clipper trails a band of rocket blast as it moves through the orbital plane, symbolizing the technological achievement of space flight.

The lunar surface is sewn in shades of light grey and tan. This gives a very striking appearance to the emblem. It makes the moon appear to be three-dimensional, rising from the surface of the patch. The lighter tan seems to be low ground, rising up to the darker greys. Indeed, the grey areas are oversewn slightly, so that the dimensional effect is not totally an illusion. In space, beyond the moon, four stars can be seen shining in space, one brighter than the other three. These stars represent the astronauts of Apollo 12. The three lighter ones are for Conrad, Gordon and Bean. The single bright one represents C. C. Williams, who was originally scheduled to be the Lunar Module Pilot on this mission. However, Williams was killed in a plane crash in 1967, and Al Bean took his place. Bean is generally credited with having the idea of putting Williams's star in the patch.

The most common souvenir version of the Apollo 12 patch is a 3" diameter emblem. Its background is a mustard-yellow twill. The border is sewn with gold mylar in an overlock style. The mission designation and crew names are sewn in royal blue, as they are in the official version. The same lunar orbit scene is depicted, although with much less detail and some variance in color. There are two glitches in the souvenir patch which are worthy of note. First, the American flag is missing from the foremast of the Yankee Clipper. Secondly, there are five stars sewn into the background, not four, as in the official emblem. Obviously, the designer of this version of the emblem did not understand the significance of the stars.

Apollo 13 carried James Lovell, Jack Swigert and Fred Haise into space on April 11, 1970. Lovell was the mission's Commander, Swigert was Command Pilot, and Haise was the Lunar Module Pilot. Originally, Tom Mattingly was scheduled to be the Command Pilot for this mission. However, Lovell, Haise and Mattingly were exposed to German measles shortly before the flight. Mattingly had no immunity to the disease and was replaced by his backup, Jack Swigert.

This was to be the third moon landing mission of the Apollo series. It was the first of three missions that were to be devoted to geological studies of the lunar surface. Launch went smoothly, as did the burn for Translunar Injection (TLI). The spacecraft was about 200,000 miles out from earth when trouble began.

The astronauts had just finished a television transmission, and were chatting with Mission Control for advice on locating Comet Bennett when Swigert interrupted: "Hey, we've got a problem here."

Nearly 56 hours into the mission, an explosion ripped the spacecraft's service module. There was an immediate drop in electrical voltage in the

Command Module, and the astronauts reported that they could see "a gas of some sort" venting into space. It was soon discovered that one of the oxygen tanks had ruptured and the "gas" was the oxygen for the Command Module.

The astronauts abandoned their Command Module and took refuge in the Lunar Module, which had its own oxygen and power supply. The immediate danger to the astronauts was a lack of sufficient oxygen for the return journey to earth. Ground technicians worked feverishly to calculate ways to conserve power and air so the crippled spacecraft could come home. Apollo 13 had become our first emergency in space.

The damaged spacecraft made a pass around the moon, using its gravity as a "slingshot" to return to earth. The crew remained in the LEM, shivering from the cold as a result of the power outage and keeping activity to a minimum to conserve oxygen. When Apollo 13 regained earth orbit, the crew transferred back into the Command Module, because the LEM was not capable of making an earth landing. The LEM and Service Module were jettisoned and the Command Module was able to safely re-enter and land. Only after the Service Module was jettisoned did the crew know the extent of the damage. As it fell to earth, the astronauts took photographs which show one entire side of the module ripped open by the force of the blast. Apollo 13 became our first space rescue mission.

The Apollo 13 patch is particularly beautiful. It is a round, 4″ diameter emblem. The border is silver mylar, sewn in overlock style. The background is black twill. Embroidered at the top of the emblem is Apollo XIII, the mission designation. At the lower left, following the edge of the patch is the phrase *Ex luna, scientia*. The translation from Latin means, *From the moon, knowledge*. An orange sun fills the background, symbolizing the task of the Apollo of Greek mythology—to pull the sun across the sky. Three horses pull Apollo's chariot and his burden. They symbolize the three astronauts of NASA's Apollo. Below the horses, a grey lunar surface rises up to meet the travellers. Far in the background, the earth rises above the moon's horizon. A vector trails from earth to the horses, symbolizing the flight path of the mission.

The Apollo 13 patch gains much of its beauty from the exquisite detail of its central symbol, the horses of Apollo. They are each a different color: a yellow roan, a tan and the familiar dark brown. The stitching is oversewn to add depth and dimension to their bodies, providing a very effective three-dimensional aspect. These steeds seem to rise right out of the emblem, as if they are about to fly past your shoulder. The trailing vector also has layered stitching, gradually getting thicker until it is built to the thickness of the horses. This also adds to the three-dimensional effect, as the vector seems to actually follow the horses' journey.

The souvenir version of the Apollo 13 patch is a round, 3″ diameter emblem. More than most, this patch stays very true to the colors and design of the official version. Like the official patch, the souvenir emblem has a silver mylar, overlock border. It has the same black twill background, and the same white lettering. There are minor differences in the shading of the three horses, but these are discernible only with a studied view. Like the 3″ Apollo 11, this patch belongs in any complete collection of space emblems.

January 31, 1971 saw the launch of Apollo 14. The crew included Alan Shepard, America's first man in space (Commander), Stuart Roosa (Command Pilot), and Ed Mitchell (Lunar Module Pilot). After the near-tragedy of Apollo 13, NASA was determined that Apollo 14 should be a resounding success. A second mishap could have caused the end of lunar (and space) exploration, when it had barely begun.

Their worst nightmare almost came true. After launch, the Command Module separated from the LEM, reversed and prepared to dock. This was the normal procedure for flight from earth orbit to the moon. Each time the two spacecraft approached and attempted to dock, the capture latches refused to operate. After four futile attempts, the astronauts were prepared to make an EVA in an attempt to solve the problem. Finally, on the fifth try, the latches held, and it was a go for the TLI. Once in lunar orbit, the two craft separated; Roosa staying behind in the Command Module, while Shepard and Mitchell headed for the lunar surface in the LEM.

Once again, problems began to appear. The landing computer was not working properly, and the landing was nearly aborted. Shepard took manual control and was able to bring the LEM down safely.

Before lift-off from the moon, Shepard produced two golf balls from his utility pouch. Using the handle of a sample retriever, he teed off, much to the amusement of those watching their television sets back on earth. Even today, this incident is cited by critics as an example of "wastefulness" of the space program, who complain about the high cost of sending a man to the moon "so he could play golf."

Shepard and Mitchell performed two EVA's on the moon, setting up several experiments and gathering more than 95 pounds of moon rocks to bring back to earth. On the return flight to earth, Mitchell conducted experiments in ESP with "listeners" on earth. This was also the last Lunar mission to require that the astronauts be quarantined upon their return to earth.

The official Apollo 14 patch is a 4", oval emblem. Like most of the official patches, it is fully embroidered. The border is an overlock style, sewn in brown. An inner band encircles the patch in gold thread. The astronauts' names are embroidered in the lower portion of this band in royal-blue thread. At the top, the band contains the mission designation, Apollo 14, sewn in brown thread.

A small inner band of white separates the patch wording from the spacescape represented in the center of the emblem. This scene is sewn with a deep royal-blue background to represent outer space. Dominating the upper left area is a detailed moon. It is sewn in black, royal blue, white and grey.

The surface detail is excellent, depicting a number of craters and other surface features. Below, and in the background, a small earth can be seen. It, too, is sewn in black, blue, grey and white, with brown added to detail the land masses. As is usual, the North and South American continents are readily identifiable.

The right half of the scene features an astronaut pin, insignia of the astronaut corps. The astronaut pin is a five-pointed star, trailing three vectors which symbolize flight trajectory (and here, the three astronauts, as well). The vectors are surrounded by an ellipse, which symbolizes orbital flight. The vectors of the pin trail completely back to earth, symbolizing the flight path of Apollo 14. The pin, and the trailing vectors, are sewn in yellow gold.

The 3" souvenir patch has the same border color and type as the official 4". The first inner band is sewn with gold mylar rather than light gold. The astronauts' names and the mission designation are located as they are in the 4" patch but are sewn with different shades of thread. In addition, there is less detail in both the earth and lunar surfaces. Both are sewn with fewer colors than the 4" version. The background of the 3" patch is a bright royal gold, much lighter in shade than the official version. Finally, the other major difference is in the astronaut pin. The souvenir version outlines the pin and trajectories in white thread. The pin itself is sewn with gold mylar, to match the outer ring.

Apollo 14 also has an unofficial 4" patch, patterned after the official version. It has a humorous theme, which incorporates the cartoon characters Roadrunner and Wile E. Coyote. The design is a take-off from the official emblem. The patch is oval and has a silver mylar, overlock border. It has an inner band of gold, encircling a thin band of white, just as the official emblem does. Embroidered at the top are the words Beep Beep. At the bottom are three names, sewn in light blue: Cernan, Evans and Engle. Gene Cernan, Ron Evans and Joe Engle were the backup crew for Apollo 14.

The interior spacescape has a royal-blue, felt background. The moon and earth are embroidered in much the same way as they are on the official mission patch. However, the cartoon characters dominate the center design in a most terrific way. Wile E. Coyote is seen blazing moonward from earth. He is sewn into the area where the astronaut pin is located in the official version. He trails three vectors, sewn in gold, in a manner similar to the pin. A white rocket blast comes from his mouth as he gazes with bloodshot eyes at the lunar orb. Standing on the moon's surface, the Roadrunner plants an American flag with his left wing, as he waves a banner with his right. Inscribed on the banner are the words 1st Team. The Roadrunner is sewn with white thread overall. Detail is added with black. His feet are yellow, and his nose is red, as is his tongue (which is sticking out at Coyote). Wile E. is sewn with brown overall, and has a white stomach. Facial detail is added with black thread to form his mouth, eyes and nose. Red lines in his eyes create the bloodshot effect.

The exact story behind the Beep Beep patch is

not known. Apparently, the Roadrunner and his 1st Team banner represent the actual crew of Apollo 14. Wile E. represents the backup crew. Since the 1st Team was able to make their flight to the moon, they are apparently having a bit of fun, teasing the three backup astronauts.

The cartoon characters suggest that Cernan, Evans and Engle could never "catch" Shepard, Roosa and Mitchell; hence the theme and the patch's name. The Roadrunner always says, "Beep Beep," just as he is about to leave Wile E. Coyote in his dust!

No one at the patch's manufacturer can remember for certain who designed and commissioned the emblem. It is thought that perhaps the 1st Team commissioned it originally, as a prank. It is also believed that a number of these patches were secreted in the Apollo 14 Command Module as unauthorized cargo, and "discovered" only after the mission had launched. The patch is still produced today, although it is not as readily available as most of the Space Program's patches.

Apollo 15 was launched from Cape Kennedy on July 26, 1971. The entire crew were Air Force personnel and included Dave Scott (Commander), Al Worden (Command Module Pilot) and Jim Irwin (Lunar Module Pilot). This was the first of three J Series missions which were intended to explore the scientific potential of the Apollo spacecraft and hardware. It was the second longest of the moon missions and the first to use the Lunar Rover, a solar-powered vehicle, designed to travel on the moon's rough surface. Apollo 15 was also one of the most trouble-free of the Apollo missions. Experiments in the Service Module, the LEM, and on the Lunar surface—all performed as hoped.

Experiments in the orbiting Service Module mapped the moon's surface, took panoramic photography, monitored solar X-ray interaction and particle emissions, and ejected a subsatellite into lunar orbit for future moon studies.

There were some problems deploying the Lunar Rover, but it worked very well. Irwin and Scott found that seat belts were essential due to the moon's light gravity. They described the ride as similar to being on the back of a "real bucking bronco."

The astronauts' second EVA proved to be very exciting. Part of the Apollo 15 mission was an attempt to locate geological samples dating from the moon's formation. Scott found a piece of anorthosite rock, which was thought to be just such a sample. It was quickly dubbed the Genesis Rock. Later, it was decided that the sample was 4,150 million years old, 150 million years older than any previous sample recovered; but unfortunately, not as old as the moon itself.

Scott set the television camera on the Lunar Rover very carefully, so that, for the first time, the launch from the lunar surface could be observed. Television screens exploded in red and green as the ascent stage of the LEM shot upwards to rendezvous with the Command Module.

Afterwards, Worden made the first spacewalk of a practical nature, when he left the spacecraft to retrieve film cassettes from the SIMBAY (Scientific Instrument Module Bay). After re-entry, one of the three capsule parachutes failed to deploy properly and did not open. The astronauts prepared for a hard landing in the water, but escaped without injury. The reason for the parachute failure was never clearly established, although it was suspected that residual fuel burning through the shroud lines may have been the cause. On later missions, fuel was not dumped, but retained on board, in an attempt to prevent further problems.

The official patch for Apollo 15 is quite pretty. The emblem is round and has a 4" diameter. The basic color scheme is red, white, and blue. The border is an overlock style and is sewn in royal blue. Just inside the border is a circle of white, containing the crew names and mission designation. These are sewn in black. Just inside the white circle is a red one, completely the patriotic flavor.

The center of the patch is dominated by a moonscape sewn in grey, silver and black thread. Flying above the moon are red, white and blue vectors. These vectors are meant to symbolize three stylized birds. They represent the crew, the number of astronauts, and the name of the Lunar Module for this mission, *Falcon*. Most of the work in this design was done by fashion designer Emilio Pucci. His concept of the patch colors were greens, blues, purples, etc. The astronauts changed the colors but used the basic design he provided. Just behind the birds on the moon's surface, a Roman numeral XV is sewn into the patch with black thread. The moonscape depicts the Apollo 15 landing site in Hadley Rille, where

Falcon planted one landing gear in a small crater, making the LEM tilt about 10° off the horizontal.

A souvenir version of Apollo 15 is made in a 3" diameter. It has a white twill ring in place of the fully embroidered one found in the official patch. However, except for its size and background material, it duplicates the original quite well. It has the same border, inner red ring, and moonscape, as the official version.

April 16, 1972, saw the launch of Apollo 16. This mission was the fifth moon landing, and, like Apollo 15, was tremendously successful. The mission got off to a rocky start as a number of technical problems kept the astronauts busy on the outbound flight. Commander John Young, Command Pilot Ken Mattingly, and Lunar Module Pilot Charles Duke, spent a great deal of time doing "home repairs" to various pieces of equipment. The major problem occurred after the undocking of the LEM in lunar orbit number twelve.

Mattingly had to fire the Command Module's main engine to correct its orbit and be available for rescue maneuvers before the LEM could attempt a landing. There were indications of yaw oscillations (possible fluctuations from axis rotation which could cause the spacecraft to tumble) in the engine's backup system. Young and Duke were given the first "space wave-off" with only minutes to go before beginning their final descent. Both spacecraft were told to continue orbiting and to reduce the distance between them in the event redocking was required. Mission Control studied the problem, and there was even talk of using the Lunar Module as a liferaft to tow the disabled Command Module back to earth, as had been done with Apollo 13. However, on the fifteenth orbit, Houston's director, Chris Kraft, gave a "go" for landing. Mattingly fired the primary engine system, and was able to successfully make his orbit more circular. The landing then proceeded uneventfully.

Three EVA's on the moon allowed the astronauts plenty of time to perform experiments and further test the Lunar Rover. John Young drove it in a planned "Grand Prix," going full speed in circles, and skidding it to test wheel grip.

The main Command Module engine burned well, in spite of the apparent malfunction of the backup. The return flight was relatively quiet, although the capsule floated upside down after splashdown until balloons were released.

The official patch for Apollo 16 is perhaps the most military looking of all the Apollo patches. It has a gold, overlock border, and is 4" in diameter. The background material is a dark-royal twill, which forms a band of blue just inside the emblem border. The astronauts' surnames are sewn in white at the bottom of the patch. Sixteen white stars are sewn into the band around the circumference of the patch, representing the flight designation of this mission.

The center of the emblem is dominated by a bald eagle perched on an American shield. The eagle and shield symbolize the United States. The eagle is sewn in brown and gold, with a white head. The shield is, of course, sewn in red, white and blue. Apollo 16 is sewn into the blue top of the shield with white thread. A gold vector sweeps across the shield, symbolizing NASA and space flight. The moon forms a globe in the center of the patch, providing an attractive silver background for the patriotic symbols. It is sewn in silver and gray thread, which gives the effect of a very bright, full moon.

The souvenir patch of Apollo 16 has a gold overlock border just like the official one. It also has the same blue twill background. However, the astronauts' names are sewn in larger size, proportionate to the patch. The result of this is that one of the sixteen stars is deleted from the outer edge of the patch. Naturally, this eliminates the symbolic intent of the stars. In this 3" emblem, they become merely aesthetic design.

The 3" patch also differs from the official in several other areas. First, the American shield is sewn a bit differently. The twill material forms the blue band at the top of the shield. In addition, a red border outlines the entire shield, which does not occur in the official version. The eagle is also slightly different, as well, since he is sewn with fewer colors. The front of his wings is sewn in gold to match the patch border, not in a darker gold as in the 4" version. Also, the vector extending across the patch face is sewn in the same gold as the border. These color changes result in lowered manufacturing costs, which help keep the retail emblem price at a lower level than that of the official emblems.

Apollo 17 was the last of the manned moon landings. It was also the one with the fewest problems. Apollo 17 was launched from Cape Kennedy on December 6, 1972. The crew were

Gene Cernan (Commander), Ron Evans (Command Module Pilot) and Jack Schmitt (Lunar Module Pilot). Dr. Schmitt was the first trained geologist to visit the moon. Apollo 17's crew stayed longer, travelled farther, and brought back more lunar samples than any other lunar mission. Apollo 17 was also America's first manned night launch of a space mission. After landing on the moon, the astronauts deployed ALSEP packages, performed heat-flow experiments, and made extensive use of the Lunar Rover. The return to earth was uneventful, ending the moon exploration program on a very successful note.

Like many of its counterparts, the official patch of the Apollo 17 moon flight is a round, 4" diameter emblem. The border is an overlock style, sewn in white. A band of grey embroidery encircles the outer edge of the emblem, containing the mission designation at the top, and the astronauts' names at the bottom. All of the lettering is sewn in white thread.

The interior of the patch depicts a scene with a number of symbolic elements. The background is embroidered with navy thread, symbolizing the reaches of deep space. In the foreground, a bust of the Greek god Apollo is sewn in gold and brown thread. Apollo is depicted in the style of classic Greek sculpture. He symbolizes NASA's Apollo program, and is sewn in gold to denote the golden age of space. Apollo looks forward, to the future, as he gazes at the planet Saturn and the spiral galaxy which are sewn just above his shoulder. This is meant to suggest that man's future still lies ahead, in the stars and planets. Saturn's main body and rings are sewn in light blue. The spiral galaxy is also sewn in light blue, and highlighted with white.

The moon is visible in the upper edge of the inner scene. It, too, is sewn with gold and brown thread to underscore the theme of the golden age. A stylized eagle's wings intersect the moon, symbolizing man's (and America's) first encounter with a celestial body. Like Apollo, the eagle is looking forward, into the future, searching for the next frontier in space. The eagle is outlined in light-blue thread and contains four red bars in his wings. The blue background forms navy bars, spaced between the red. These bars represent the United States and its flag, just as the eagle implies our national heritage. Three white stars represent the crew of Apollo 17. Their location also helps to complete the flag symbolism in the eagle's wings.

The souvenir version of the patch is a round, 3" diameter emblem. Like the official version, it has a white border and a grey inner band of embroidery. The mission designation and the astronauts' names are sewn in white. The inner band, which forms the background for the names is lighter in color than the official emblem. The 4" patch has a definite grey band. In the 3", the grey is so light as to be almost a shade of silver.

The outline of the eagle is sewn in white thread, eliminating the light blue seen in the official patch. This is also true of the spiral galaxy and Saturn, as well. It should also be noted that the smaller patch size makes it much more difficult to sew the detail in the celestial bodies. They are not as readily identifiable as they are in the official version. Other colors in the 3" emblem duplicate the 4" quite well. The golds and browns of the moon and Apollo are repeated, as are the navy-blue background and red bars.

5 ▪ THE SKYLAB PROGRAM

Skylab was America's first space station. For the first time in our space program, astronauts had an environment suitable for extended habitation in the hazardous environs of outer space. A major goal of Skylab was to study the physical effects caused by flights of long duration. Other goals included studies of solar activity without the interference of earth's atmosphere, and the study of earth itself from the vantage point of earth orbit. Earth studies were to concentrate on natural resources, pollution problems, and natural disasters such as floods, storms, earthquakes and volcanic eruptions.

Skylab was launched from Cape Kennedy by a Saturn 5 rocket on May 14, 1973, and was subsequently "visited" and manned by three different crews of Apollo astronauts who lived and worked in it for extended periods, despite certain problems that were created during the launch of the space station itself.

Skylab was a remarkable example of NASA's ability to improvise and overcome major technical snafus. Although the space station achieved its proper orbit, launch vibrations had ripped away the meteoroid/thermal shield, which, in turn, tore away one of the pair of solar array wings. The other pair were jammed partly open by debris.

Temperatures inside Skylab soared without thermal protection from the shield. Loss of the solar arrays left the station with limited power which was then provided only by the Apollo Telescope Mount (ATM) batteries. This created several major problems for any human inhabitants. First, without the shield, Skylab was vulnerable to meteorite damage and was unprotected from the incredible force of the sun. The high temperatures generated made Skylab uninhabitable unless repairs could be made. The damage and loss of the solar arrays also meant that Skylab might lack electrical power, which would also render it uninhabitable. The space station depended on solar energy to charge batteries for life-support systems, experiments, and other scientific equipment. If the solar arrays could not be replaced or repaired, the loss of the thermal shield made little difference.

The first crew of Skylab was to have launched within twenty-four hours of the Skylab, and take up immediate residence. Their launch was quickly postponed when the station's problems became apparent. At first, it seemed that Skylab would remain uninhabitable, since internal temperatures soared to highs of 190 degrees Fahrenheit. However, Mission Control learned to orient the array cluster at the most favorable angle to the sun, which allowed the internal temperature to stabilize at a much lower level.

Finally, two methods were devised to replace the Skylab's thermal shield. First, an umbrella-like sunscreen would be deployed by pushing it from inside the space station through one of the airlocks, and then opening it. Then, a twin-pole screen could be pushed back over the station during an EVA. In addition, two astronauts would attempt to extend the jammed solar array by standing in the Command Module and pulling it with a pole. Ultimately, these activities were successful, and Skylab proved to be an excellent laboratory in space.

The official program patch for Skylab is known as the Skylab USA. It is a round patch, 4" in diameter. It is a fully embroidered emblem, with a light-green overlock border. An inner band of light green is sewn inside the border. In this band, at the bottom of the emblem, is sewn United States of America, in white. A small white circle encloses an artistic rendering of the Skylab in orbit.

The space station is depicted in earth orbit with the sun in the background. The earth is sewn in shades of blue ranging from very light to navy. The space station itself is embroidered in much the same color scheme, although white and black thread are added for detail. The sun has a bright yellow center and emits orange rays in a burst pattern. The background is sewn with deep navy to represent space. The project name, Skylab, is sewn to the right of the sun in yellow gold.

A 3" souvenir version of the program patch follows the design closely. The border and inner band duplicate the light-green shading of the official emblem. The background is a navy twill, set against the Skylab itself. The space station is sewn almost completely in royal blue, with white and black adding detail. Fewer shades of blue are used in the earth, and white is added, which adds a cloud effect in the earth's atmosphere. The sun's colors are reversed. That is, orange forms the center and yellow the burst effect. The program name is sewn in the same orange as the center of the sun.

The first manned Skylab mission lasted twenty-eight days in earth orbit. The three-man crew included Charles Conrad, a former Gemini and Apollo astronaut; Paul Weitz, and Dr. Joseph Kerwin. Launch was by a Saturn 1B, which lifted the Apollo Command Module and Service module into orbit for rendezvous with Skylab. After many futile attempts to dock with Skylab, Mission Control began to give serious thought to an emergency return to earth for the crew. But the astronauts refused to give up. After the third EVA in one day, Conrad was finally able to complete the docking maneuver.

While Conrad rested in the Command Module, Kerwin and Weitz tested the Skylab for dangerous gases and opened the hatches to the Multiple Docking Adapter, the Airlock Module, and the Orbital Workshop. Later, Conrad and Weitz slowly forced the "umbrella" shield through a scientific airlock. The wrinkles and folds were smoothed out and the handle was pulled back into Skylab, section by section, until the sunscreen rested snugly just above the workshop. Now that it was protected from the sun, the space station finally began to cool.

The astronauts' next task was to attempt a repair of the damaged solar panels, which provided power to the still crippled Skylab. Kerwin and Conrad donned spacesuits and went outside on their ninth day, to cut away the damaged heat shield and free the remaining solar panel so that it could be fully extended. After some difficulty, the solar array was freed and extended. Power began to flow to Skylab's electrical batteries almost immediately. By the end of the twenty-eight-day mission, the solar wing was producing more than 5,500 watts of power, more than enough for the entire mission.

During their stay in Skylab, the crew of Skylab 1 made many solar observations. They were able to study a solar flare, take many photographs of earth, and recover data about natural resources and geology from around the globe. Data was obtained over 31 U.S. states, 6 foreign countries, the Pacific Ocean, Atlantic Ocean, and the other oceans. Almost all of the problems caused by launch had been repaired. The crew of Skylab I left a clean and working home for the next group of astronauts scheduled to man the station.

The official Skylab I patch was designed by science fiction illustrator Kelly Freas. It is a round, 4" diameter emblem, and is fully embroidered. The patch has an overlock border, sewn with black thread. A thin white circle forms a band directly inside the border of the emblem.

The patch shows the Skylab silhouetted against the earth's globe. In turn, the earth is eclipsing the sun, thus showing the brilliant signet-ring pattern of that small instant before total eclipse occurs. Skylab I is sewn in black at the top of the emblem. The bold black letters are outlined in white. At the bottom, the astronauts' surnames are sewn in white. The silhouette of the Skylab is also sewn in black, with white and light blue added for highlight and detail.

The earth is depicted as the "big blue marble," with no land masses visible. Swirls of light and royal blue give the impression of the earth as seen from a long distance in space. The globe is outlined in white, as if the sun is creating a corona as it is eclipsed by the earth. The starburst effect is embroidered with white, gold, tan, brown and orange. It radiates throughout the background of the emblem, creating a brilliant spectrum of color.

A souvenir version of the patch is made in a round 3″ diameter size. It duplicates the colors of the official emblem very closely. Some of the detail is not as sharp as the official version, but this can mainly be ascribed to the smaller size. The souvenir version is an excellent collectible.

The second manned Skylab mission was launched on July 28, 1973. The crew included Al Bean (Commander), Owen Garriott (Science Pilot) and Jack Lousma (Pilot). The Apollo spacecraft was able to dock with Skylab without mishap. The first two days of the mission were spent switching on lights, air-conditioning and power systems.

All three astronauts developed spacesickness due to the weightless conditions and this caused a delay in moving their cargo and stores from the Command Module to Skylab itself. This cargo included white mice, minnows and two spiders (named Anita and Arabella). A major crisis occurred on the fifth day, when a leak developed in a Command Module thruster. This meant that the maneuvering ability of the Apollo spacecraft could be greatly diminished. An emergency return was considered, while enough fuel remained, but the idea was discarded. Instead, Mission Control chose to prepare a rescue mission, which would fly two astronauts up to Skylab to retrieve the three crew members already there. This would allow the Skylab crew to carry out their program of experiments, without jeopardizing their safety. Ultimately, engineers on the ground were able to develop procedures that permitted the Apollo spacecraft to provide a safe return to earth. Thus, the rescue operation was never needed.

Had it been necessary, the spacecraft for Skylab 3 would have been prepared for launch, and used as a rescue vehicle. Launch procedures would have taken an estimated 35 days, so this action would only have been taken as a last resort. In effect, a two-man crew would have flown up to Skylab, retrieving the three stranded astronauts and bringing them back to earth. This option did allow the crew of Skylab 2 to complete most of the mission objectives, so it was chosen as the best alternative (the astronauts were in no danger while staying in Skylab). Ultimately, the Skylab 2 spacecraft performed well, and the rescue mission became unnecessary.

Much was accomplished during the mission of Skylab II. A new sun shield was deployed as a backup to the "umbrella." Studies were done on the spiders, observing the effects of weightlessness on their ability to spin a web. They were seemingly not bothered at all by a lack of gravity. The astronauts also successfully tested Astronaut Maneuvering Units (AMUs) for use during future spacewalks. In addition, Skylab II brought back 75,000 photos of the sun (which included photography of six solar flares), photographs and tapes of 26 earth-resources (EREP) orbits, and the results of numerous welding and materials-processing experiments. Skylab II also provided much medical data about the long-term effects of living in a space environment, which was one of its primary objectives.

The official patch of Skylab II is one of the most beautiful in the history of the Space Program. The basic color scheme is red, white and blue. These colors, of course, are representative of the United States. The emblem is a round 4″ diameter patch. The border is a red, overlock style. Inside the border is a white, and then a royal-blue, band. The border and these two bands set an immediate tone for the color scheme of the patch. The background of the patch is white and is fully embroidered. The astronauts' names are sewn with black thread in an arc at the top. At the bottom, the mission designation, Skylab II, is also sewn in black.

The patch symbolizes the main objectives of the Spacelab II mission. The central figure is adapted from one by Leonardo da Vinci and illustrates the proportions of the human form. It is also meant to suggest the many studies of man himself which are to be conducted in the zero-gravity environment of space. The figure is sewn in white, with detail and outline in black. The use of da Vinci's drawing is particularly apropos for this patch. In his day, he was a major scientist, engineer and thinker, as well as a great artist. His studies included astronomy, aerodynamics, hydraulics and anatomy; and his concepts and designs were far ahead of their time.

Da Vinci's man is superimposed onto two hemispheres which represent the two additional main areas of Skylab research: studies of the sun, and the development of techniques for survey of the earth's resources.

The left hemisphere shows the sun as it is seen in the red light radiated by hydrogen atoms in the solar atmosphere. On the solar surface, the patch depicts filaments and active regions, such as solar flares. These are sewn in orange thread with black detail. The right hemisphere suggests the studies of earth resources, which were conducted on Skylab. These studies were done with photography and electronic imaging, and have been used to evaluate and develop the manufacturing and usage potential of Earth's land and water. Thus the blue oceans and grey land masses symbolize this photography and imaging processes.

The souvenir version of Skylab II is also very well done. It differs from the official in size, as most do. It is a 3" diameter emblem. The background is white twill, not embroidery; but the beauty and brilliance of the design is true to the official patch. The colors of the border, the sun and the earth duplicate those used in the official patch. Da Vinci's figure does lose some detail, due mainly to the smaller size of the emblem. The overall quality and look of the souvenir version are quite good, however, and it should be considered a must for any complete collection.

The launch of Skylab 3's crew was six days late, due to fatigue cracks in the Saturn 1B's fins. It was finally launched on November 16, 1973. The mission duration was 84 days, a record time-span at the time, for a weightless mission in space. The crew were Commander Gerald Carr, Science Pilot Dr. Ed Gibson, and Pilot William Pogue.

One of the main objectives of Skylab 3 was to observe the comet Kohoutek, which had been discovered the previous March and only orbited near the earth and sun every 80,000 years. It was thought at the time that this would be the biggest astronomical event since Halley's comet had last arrived in 1910. Two EVA's were made to mount cameras on the ATM. These were to provide pictures of the comet's changing composition as it became heated by the sun. Unfortunately, Kohoutek did not live up to its promise as a major astronomical event, although the crew was able to collect much data.

On December 18, 1973, the Soviet Union launched Soyuz 13 on an eight-day flight, marking the first time that American astronauts and Russian cosmonauts were in space together. No direct communications were possible between the spacemen, and neither crew reported sighting the other. When the astronauts finally undocked from Skylab to return to earth, they were making their 1,213th orbit of earth. Skylab was completing orbit number 3,898. During a final fly-around the crew reported that both sunshades were faded, and one had developed a split. Mission Control depressurized Skylab from the ground, and it was a dead space station by the time her last crew had landed on earth.

Skylab's orbit gradually decayed and it fell back to earth on July 11, 1979. It disintegrated in the atmosphere, although some debris did come to earth in western Australia. Much of this debris was recovered and turned over to NASA for study. Later, these pieces were returned to the people who found them as souvenirs of Skylab.

The official patch of the Skylab 3 mission is shaped like a triangle with rounded corners. Like most official emblems, it is fully embroidered. The border is an overlock style, and is sewn in light blue. The embroidered background is also a matching shade of blue. The upper side of the triangle designates the patch as Skylab in navy-blue thread. A large "3" is sewn in navy on the right side of the patch. At the bottom, the astronauts' names are sewn in white.

The symbols in the patch are indicative of the three major areas of investigation for this mission. The tree represents man's natural environment and relates directly to the Skylab mission objectives of advancing the study of earth resources. The hydrogen atom is the basic building block of the universe, and represents man's exploration of the physical world, his application of knowledge, and his development of technology. The sun is composed primarily of hydrogen, and therefore the atom also symbolizes the solar physics mission objectives. The human silhouette represents humankind and the human capacity to direct technology with a wisdom tempered by regard for his natural environment. It is, at the same time, a symbol of the Skylab medical studies of man himself. The rainbow was adopted from the biblical story of the flood and symbolizes the promise that is offered to man. It embraces man and extends to the tree and the atom, emphasizing man's pivotal role in the conciliation between technology and nature.

The souvenir version of Skylab 3 is a 3″ patch. It has a light-blue twill background with a matching overlock border. It contains the same symbols as the original, although they are sewn with fewer colors. For example, the interior of the 3 is sewn with the same grey as the interior of the rainbow. On the official version, the 3 has a white interior, sewn with vertical stitching. It is only shaded slightly with grey on the interior curves. The rainbow has the same colors in both versions, but they are sewn in different sequence in the souvenir emblem. The leaves of the tree are sewn with a blue-green thread in the 3″ patch. The official version has leaves of kelly green and light blue.

The successful completion of the Skylab missions marked the end of the first era of manned spaceflight in the United States. Many Americans doubted whether Skylab was worth the more than $2,000,000,000 (two billion) it had cost. However, the earth-resources equipment located many mineral deposits that had heretofore gone undiscovered. One copper deposit that was uncovered is estimated to be worth many billions of dollars in excess of the cost of the *entire* American space program to date. Even with all its problems, Skylab achieved more than was hoped for if it had worked perfectly.

Skylab also effectively demonstrated man's adaptability. The last crew (Skylab 3) flew the longest mission in Skylab, yet returned to earth in the best physical condition. Proof that man can endure long periods in space means that dreams of permanent space stations, lunar colonies, and manned missions to Mars can now become realities. Skylab also performed important defense activities for the American military. Specific events are not discussed, but the astronauts certainly made many visual observations of Soviet missile bases and activity along the Soviet/Chinese border. These sightings were as valuable as the photography and sensory data recorded by Skylab's cameras and other equipment. They ensure that astronauts will be an essential part of future military reconnaissance systems in space. One need only look to the Department of Defense payloads flown on the Space Shuttle to confirm that this is true. Shuttle crews have performed a number of military experiments. At least two flights, to date, have carried military payloads. Soon, the Military Space Command will launch regular payloads, using the Space Shuttle, from Vandenberg Air Force Base in California. In addition, the United States will soon have a permanently staffed Space Station orbiting in space.

6 ■ THE APOLLO/SOYUZ PROGRAM

Plans for a joint American/Soviet space mission were outlined and included in an agreement on the peaceful exploration of space which was signed by Soviet leader Kosygin and U.S. President Nixon on May 24, 1972. The project was later named the Apollo/Soyuz Test Project (ASTP). ASTP would mark the first (and, to date, the last) cooperative space effort by the two post-World War II adversaries. The launch date goal was set for July 15, 1975. Crews were announced some two years before launch, although the planning and preparation took nearly four years. The average age of the two crews was 45, the oldest of any spacemen up to that time. This was due partly to the political need for diplomacy, as well as the mission requirements for experience in space travel.

Commander of the U.S. crew was Tom Stafford. Deke Slayton was the Docking Module Pilot, and Vance Brand was the Command Module Pilot. The Soviet Commander was Alexei Leonov, the first man to walk in space. His Flight Engineer was Valeri Kubasov. The flight plan called for the two crews to launch on the same day from separate locations, achieve earth orbit, rendezvous, and dock with the aid of a docking module.

Many people in the United States felt that the flight would never actually take place, due to the prevailing international political climate. These pessimists were proven wrong by several factors. Russia was emerging from a long period of setbacks and failures in its space program and wanted very badly to improve its record. The Soviets saw ASTP as an opportunity to improve their technology and methodology with American help.

In particular, the Soviets needed help in the area of quality control. Russian spacecraft had never had the technological and operational consistency of the American equipment. For this reason, Russian space scientists took pains to cooperate with their Western counterparts.

ASTP also had a number of political benefits for the United States. First, it gave American scientists an opportunity to learn about the Soviet space program. It provided staffed space flight activity during the long timespan between the completion of Skylab and the beginning of the Space Shuttle program. The American fascination with space flight was waning; and, as a result, NASA had been facing budget restraints in Congress since before the end of the Apollo program. As interest diminished, and space flight began to seem commonplace, funds for further projects became more and more difficult to obtain. American political attention was focused on domestic and international problems on earth. Issues such as poverty, civil rights, women's rights, terrorism, Viet Nam and spiraling inflation were focused sharply in the minds of the American public. Many people wanted to cure the problems we all faced here on earth. The benefits of space exploration began to seem esoteric and too long range. As a result, they needed ever-increasing justification. Finally, there was also a good deal of Apollo/Saturn hardware left over from the Apollo and Skylab programs. Letting it go to waste would only increase NASA's problems in the political arena.

The two countries jointly defined a "common interface" for their spacecraft which included seals, guide pedals, latches and structural rings. Each spacecraft's docking system for meeting this interface was designed independently. As a result, American scientists were able to design a new docking mechanism which eliminated the "docking probe." The probe had been a source of trouble throughout the Apollo program. This new docking system was the one major technical advance of the mission, since NASA elected to use it on future Space Shuttle missions. The docking assembly was constructed in the United States and jointly tested by Soviet and NASA engineers.

The Docking Module was basically an airlock with docking equipment at each end. This allowed the spacemen to move back and forth between the Soyuz and Apollo spacecraft. It contained control and display panels, radio equipment, storage areas and life-support equipment. This included such gear as fire extinguishers, oxygen masks, handholds, communication linkages, floodlights, and TV equipment. The Docking Module also housed the Multipurpose Electric Furnace, which allowed the two crews to conduct high-pressure experiments.

The launch countdown was one of the most complex in the history of space exploration. It had to be coordinated between the Apollo launch site in Florida, and the Soyuz site in Russia. The Russian Soyuz 19 was launched on July 15, 1975, followed some seven and one-half hours later by the Apollo. The last Saturn 1B carried the American craft into orbit. This launch sequence marked the first time that a Soviet launch was seen on live television.

Both crews experienced technical problems, but none serious enough to put the mission in jeopardy. The two craft docked on their first attempt on July 17. In a grand gesture of international cooperation, it was agreed that each crew would speak the other's language (it was estimated that the American spacemen spent over 1,000 hours learning Russian, in preparation for the event). Three hours after docking the Soyuz hatch was opened and handshakes took place. President Ford and Soviet leader Brezhnev offered mutual congratulations amid a good deal of confused communications.

While in orbit the two crews worked together, ate together and visited each other's spacecraft. They also held a television news conference and carried out joint experiments in the Docking Module. Apollo's normal atmosphere in orbit was 100% oxygen while the Soyuz spacecraft used an oxygen/nitrogen mixture at 14.7 lb./sq. in. For this reason, the cosmonauts had to spend as much as two hours in the docking module before entering the Apollo capsule. During this time they pre-breathed oxygen to purge suspended nitrogen from their bloodstreams. This activity prevented the cosmonauts from developing what deep-sea divers call the bends. When the Soviets agreed to lower their cabin pressure, transfers between the two craft could be made "in shirtsleeves." The Docking Module system was always operated by an Apollo astronaut, with two men in the module during a transfer. The ground rules stated that one cosmonaut would always be in the Soyuz and one astronaut in the Apollo. This was a safety measure designed to provide expedient action should pressurization problems occur. There were hatches at both ends of the Docking Module equipped with pressure-equalization valves. These hatches made it possible to transfer between the two spacecraft without disturbing the atmosphere in either. The spacecraft remained joined together for 43 hours before separating for the return to earth.

Soyuz 19 re-entered on its 96th orbit and touched down (again with live television coverage) in Kazakhstan. It had flown in space for 5 days, 22 hours and 31 minutes. The Apollo capsule remained in orbit making earth-resources observations and performing other experiments. The Apollo capsule finally re-entered on orbit #138, ending a 9-day, 1-hour and 28-minute mission. Thus ended the first (and so far, the last) joint American-Soviet space mission.

There are two patches that mark the Apollo/Soyuz missions. The first is generally known as the program patch, and the latter, the crew patch.

In fact, the program patch was designed by the Soviets. The official version is a round, 3½" diameter emblem, which is fully embroidered. It has an overlock border sewn in gold mylar. A center disc of white embroidery depicts the two spacecraft docked together in Earth orbit. Lines of latitude and longitude are sewn on the globe in gold. The Apollo and Soyuz spacecraft are also sewn in gold thread.

The earth is seen only as a white disc behind the two spacecraft, with no detail represented. Two crescents surround the earth, a blue one to the left, and a red one to the right. The word Apollo is embroidered in the blue field, representing the American team. In the red is the word *Soyuz*, for the Soviet team, spelled in Russian. The translation of *Soyuz* in English is union. Both Apollo and Soyuz are embroidered in gold mylar to match the emblem border. Gold mylar also forms the outline of the Earth, and is a dividing line between the red and blue fields.

Several souvenir versions of the program patch have been made. Two of the best known are pictured here. Both of them are 4″ in diameter which makes them larger than the official emblem. While they duplicate the design of the official emblem, both of the souvenir versions use slightly different colors in their formats. In the first, the border and dividing lines between the crescents are sewn in yellow gold. Yellow gold is also used to form the lines of latitude and longitude on the earth, as well as of the two spacecraft. The same color also spells out Apollo and Soyuz. The red, blue and white fields match the official emblem colors almost exactly.

The second souvenir patch also uses a different thread color to create the border, dividing lines and lettering. These areas are embroidered in a very light-gold thread. The blue and red crescents vary a good deal from those in the official patch. Both colors are darker and not as bright. In addition, the spacecraft and geographical lines are sewn in gold mylar.

The Apollo/Soyuz mission also had a crew patch which was designed by the Americans. In the official version it is a round 4″ diameter emblem with a bright-red overlock border. The Russian cosmonauts saw the design during pre-mission training and agreed that it would be the crew patch for the mission.

Sewn inside the red border is a band of gold mylar. This area contains the mission name, Apollo/Soyuz, at the top. At the bottom it includes the astronauts' and cosmonauts' names. The word Soyuz and the cosmonauts' names are spelled in Russian. All wording is sewn with black thread. The center of the patch depicts the American and Soviet spacecraft as they are about to dock. A small light-blue area breaks the gold band at the upper left side of the patch. Inside it are three white stars which symbolize the three Apollo crewmen (Stafford, Brand, Slayton). A similar area breaks the band at the upper right side of the patch. It is sewn in red (to match the border) and contains two gold mylar stars. These represent the Soviet crew members (Leonov and Kubasov). The red background in this area is symbolic of the Soviet Union. The blue, of course, represents the United States.

The earth can be seen at the bottom edge of this inner spacescape. It is sewn with white and several shades of blue. No identifiable geographical areas are visible. The background is embroidered with a deep navy blue to symbolize space. Above the two spacecraft, a bright sun radiates in hues of yellow, gold and white. The Apollo spacecraft is sewn in shades of grey and blue, which represent the actual metallic hues of the real vehicle. A light "dusting" of gold is sewn across the top, suggesting the reflection of the brilliant sunlight streaming from above. The Soviet capsule is sewn in green and grey, again symbolic of the actual colors of the spacecraft. Like the Apollo capsule, the Soyuz is "dusted" with golden rays of sunlight along its upper edge.

A 3″ diameter souvenir version of the patch duplicates the design and color of the official emblem extraordinarily well. The navy background is twill and not embroidered, but that is the only major difference other than size. The official and souvenir patches are both quite beautiful, and most certainly belong in any complete collection of space emblems. They represent a unique event in the history of man's voyages beyond the physical and political boundaries of his world. No other joint space missions have been flown by the United States and the Soviet Union, and none are currently planned. There have been international crews on several Space Shuttle missions (a Canadian, Frenchman and a Saudi-Arabian prince); and the Russians have included foreign nationals (an Indian, Vietnamese, Rumanian and Frenchman) as crew members on Salyut missions. Apollo/Soyuz remains the only space flight that saw manned craft from two countries rendezvous and dock in space as part of a joint effort. The fact that this was accomplished by political antagonists is all the more reason to celebrate the achievements of ASTP.

7 ▪ THE SPACE SHUTTLE PROGRAM

America's space program has come of age with the advent of the Shuttle Transportation System (STS). By all estimates and forecasts, the Space Shuttle will dominate the development and focus of space flight in the west for the rest of this century. This remains true even when considering the impact of the ill-fated Challenger mission (STS-51L). It is the first reusable space vehicle in our history. In addition, it is tremendously versatile. The Space Shuttle can carry large equipment in its cargo bay, such as satellites, space pods, experimental pallets, etc. It can also retrieve satellites from orbit, return them to earth for repair, and then carry them back into orbit again. It has made the prospect of a large, permanently manned space station feasible in the near future. Many futurists envision the Shuttle acting as a dependable "space truck," ferrying building material and supplies to permanent orbiting platforms, stations, and colonies.

While the conception of a reusable space vehicle was first proposed in the early 1970's, the Space Shuttle can actually trace its roots all the way back to the 1950's. It has been said that the "granddaddy" of the Space Shuttle was the X-15 rocket plane. Indeed, the X-15 was launched in the air (from the underside of a B-52), where it ignited its rocket engines and blasted skyward into the fringes of outer space. X-15 pilots escaped earth's atmosphere and experienced brief weightlessness just as the astronauts do. And, of course, the X-15 was a reusable "spacecraft." Many observers of the space program say that the X-15 would have evolved into a Space Shuttle vehicle much sooner had America not felt so compelled to enter a race to space with the Soviets. Our desire to be first on the moon slowed shuttle development for a decade or more.

After the moon landings, NASA's attention returned to the concept of a space vehicle that would have practical, workaday features. The cost of space vehicles that could only be used for one mission was not practical from a business point of view. Science fiction had long suggested that man could live and work in space. For this to be practical, he would need vehicles and equipment that performed as reliably, consistently and economically as a farmer's pick-up truck. This meant that the vehicle must be reusable, versatile, dependable and easy to fly. In addition, it would have to land on the ground, like an airplane. Water landings would not be cost effective or convenient over the long term. Even the rocket engines to launch it would have to be reusable in order to be practical and cost-effective. Until the cost of going into space was reduced, only governments could afford to do it. Only a vehicle like the Space Shuttle could lower costs, making space a practical, commercial venture.

The Shuttle Orbiters are just over 120 feet long

and nearly 57 feet tall. They have a wing span of 78 feet. They are usually described as being approximately the size of a DC-9 airliner. Original development plans called for the construction of one ground-test and five operational vehicles. These plans were later revised to four operational vehicles because of budget restraints. Before it was named, the ground-test vehicle was designated OV-099. The flight-operational vehicles were designated OV-101 to OV-105. OV-105 was never built.

The Approach and Landing Tests (ALT) began in 1977. At that time, NASA wanted to name OV-101 the *Constitution*. Over 10,000 fans of the television show *Star-Trek* wrote to President Ford in protest and asked that he name the first Orbiter *Enterprise*, after the spaceship in the TV show. Ford met with NASA Administrator James Fletcher and it was decided to give way to popular demand. This did cause some internal embarrassment at NASA, since it had been determined that OV-101 would never go into orbit. It was later decided to upgrade OV-099 so it would be the second Shuttle to fly, thus making the *Enterprise* the ground-test vehicle after the completion of the ALT program.

The first four operational Space Shuttles were then named after famous sailing ships that had pioneered exploration of the globe. OV-102 was named *Columbia*, after one of the first Navy frigates to circumnavigate the earth. This was also the name of the Apollo Command Module for the first moon landing (Apollo 11). Since OV-102 would be the first Shuttle to fly, the name was then doubly appropriate. OV-099 was dubbed *Challenger* after the ship that explored the Pacific and Atlantic in 1872 through 1876. OV-103 was named *Discovery*, for two ships. The first *Discovery* was the one in which Captain Cook discovered the Hawaiian Islands. The second was the vessel that first sailed into Hudson's Bay in 1610. The fifth Shuttle, OV-104, was named *Atlantis* after the vessel that did oceanographic research during the years 1930–1966. *Columbia* was the first Orbiter to fly, followed by *Challenger*, *Discovery* and *Atlantis*, in that order.

The original conception of the Space Shuttle called for it to be the sole United States space launcher for the 1980's and 1990's. By mid-1983 this notion had changed. Shuttle missions were no longer viewed by the Pentagon and military specialists as the only alternative for space exploitation. Indeed, the Space Shuttle competes not only with the European Space Agency's (ESA) Ariane rocket (an unmanned vehicle), but with an unmanned Titan-Centaur under development for the Air Force. The Soviet Union is also developing a very aggressive commercial space program, which is marketed to Third World and European countries. Ventures into space by the private sector and the world's nations are increasing rapidly. The Shuttle's general record of excellence makes it very often the vehicle of choice, but it is certainly not the *only* choice.

The Orbiter *Enterprise* provided the first test flights of the Space Shuttle vehicles. *Enterprise* rolled out of its final assembly facilities on September 17, 1977. The Orbiter(s) was built by Rockwell International Corporation in its Palmdale, California, plant. The *Enterprise* flew a total of thirteen Approach and Landing Tests. Some of these were "captive" flights. This meant that the Orbiter remained affixed to the 747 transport aircraft and carried no crew. Later, two-man crews would man the flight deck and check systems' performance.

In August of 1977, the first of five "free" flights began. *Enterprise* was launched from its carrier, and glided down to landings at Edwards Air Force Base in California. After the ALT tests were completed, *Enterprise* was modified for vertical ground vibration tests at Marshall Space Flight Center (in Huntsville, Alabama) and used as the test vehicle for mating tests with the External Tank (ET) and Solid Rocket Boosters (SRB).

In recent years, the *Enterprise* has toured the world, promoting the Shuttle program, and thrilling millions of people at air shows and exhibitions. Eventually, it will be displayed at the Smithsonian Institution in Washington, D.C.

The ALT program inspired the first Shuttle patch in the series. It is known as the ALT *Enterprise*, and is a round 4" diameter patch. Like most official NASA patches, it is fully embroidered. The patch has a silver ravel-proof overlock border. A thin black band is sewn just inside the border, helping to outline a wider band of white. The project name, Approach and Landing Test, is sewn in a red arc inside this white band.

The center of the emblem is dominated by a large red vector which encompasses a depiction of the Orbiter. The *Enterprise* is sewn in white thread with black detail. As with the actual vehicle, an American flag is represented on the top of the left wing. Below the Orbiter, at the bottom of the patch, the name *Enterprise* is embroidered in white.

The test flights of the *Enterprise* were flown by two crews. The prime crew consisted of Fred Haise and Gordon Fullerton. Their surnames are embroidered in white at the left edge of the vector. The names of the second crew, Joe Engle and Richard Truly, are sewn at the right edge of the vector. These two crews made alternate flights on the *Enterprise*, helping scientists make final checks on the various Shuttle systems. Engle and Truly would also become the flight crew for STS-2, the second spaceflight of the operational Shuttle series.

While the ALT patch is quite lovely and very striking, it is not as well known as the Shuttle mission patches. However, no collection of Shuttle and Shuttle-related patches would be complete without it. There is no known souvenir version of the emblem available at this writing, but the official version is readily available at NASA centers, space museums and dealers in space-patch collectibles.

Like Gemini, Apollo, Skylab and Apollo-Soyuz, the Space Shuttle Program has its own program patch. There are two official versions and one souvenir version. In its original concept, the program insignia would have been the only patch worn by Shuttle astronauts.

In December of 1976, NASA officially described the Shuttle Program patch in this way: "The emblem is triangular in shape, pointed upward with an overhead view of the Space Shuttle in white on a field of two shades of blue. The entire emblem is outlined by a gold band. The insignia represents the entire Space Transportation System or Space Shuttle program, and *there will be no separate and distinct badges for each shuttle mission* [italics added]. However, payloads, missions and other elements of a specific Shuttle activity may be identified in a separate block which may be used with the Shuttle insignia. This block will be rectangular in shape and be added to the bottom of the Shuttle insignia." This design idea continued to be the official one throughout the late 70's.

NASA's main reasons for this type of insignia were the large numbers of scheduled Shuttle missions. Original plans for the STS program called for 570 individual missions between 1980 and 1991. NASA considered that 570 individual mission patches were just too many. The number of missions has been scaled back, although as many as 312 are still planned through 1994. However, as the number of planned missions declined, the astronaut corps was determined to continue the tradition of a mission patch which had begun with Gemini 5. NASA acquiesced, and, to date, every Space Shuttle mission has had its own emblem.

As Shuttle missions grow more frequent (the eventual goal is one every two weeks), NASA rumor says that individual Shuttle mission patches will be eliminated. As a group, Shuttle patches already comprise the largest body of emblems ever made for one NASA project. Interestingly enough, Shuttle patches have introduced more people to patch-collecting and the U.S. space program than any other NASA patches.

The official Shuttle Program patch is now made in a 4" and an 8" size. The original triangular shape is still the basic form. The patch points upwards and contains an overhead view of the Shuttle mounted on the ET and SRB's. The border of the patch is a ravel-proof overlock style sewn in gold mylar. An inner band of white is sewn completely around the edge of the design.

The Shuttle is also embroidered in white, with grey added for shading and detail. A two-tone blue field forms the background, just as it was described in the initial version. The words Space Shuttle are embroidered in white at the bottom of the patch. The patch is worn by the astronauts and by NASA ground personnel. The 4" version is a shoulder or breast patch. The 8" size is generally reserved for use on the backs of jackets and lab coats. As is usual, the 4" and 8" emblems are fully embroidered.

There is also a 3" souvenir version of the Shuttle Program (also known as the Shuttle Triangle) patch. It duplicates the official emblem remarkably well, although it is not a fully embroidered patch. The upper field of the 3" version is navy twill. There are some slight color variations in the lower background field, and the detail work on the shuttle itself is not as extensive. The inner band of white is sewn with a single line of white stitching on this emblem. However, the border is gold mylar, just as it is in the official emblem.

The souvenir program patch is nearly as popular as the official version, mainly because it is used extensively on caps. The Shuttle Program insignia is almost as popular with the general public as the NASA logo when it is applied to a cap. NASA Exchanges and Visitor Centers use thousands of these emblems to meet the great demand for Space Shuttle caps.

STS-1 was the first orbital mission of a Shuttle Orbiter. The Orbiter *Columbia* was the first to fly of the four flight-operational vehicles. Indeed, *Challenger*, *Discovery* and *Atlantis* were still in various stages of construction when *Columbia* flew her first mission. The original launch date was set for April 10, 1981. Lift-off was delayed for 48 hours due to computer problems. *Columbia* left the pad for the first time at 7:00 A.M. on Sunday, April 12, 1981. That Sunday was also the twentieth anniversary of the first manned space flight, piloted by Soviet cosmonaut Yuri Gagarin. *Columbia* carried two astronauts on her maiden voyage: John Young, Commander, and Bob Crippen. As *Columbia* climbed skyward Young was moved to remark, "Flying this thing is just outstanding!"

The first flight was mainly a test of the Shuttle system's reusability, and this led to a great deal of interest in the recovery of the Solid Rocket Boosters. The SRB's landed approximately 15 miles from the recovery ships and were successfully recovered with little trouble. The Orbiter separated from the ET just as planned, and the crew made preparations for orbital insertion.

Once they were safely in orbit, Young and Crippen opened the doors to *Columbia*'s cargo bay to make sure they were working properly. Launch and the extreme temperature of space caused no problem, for the doors opened and closed perfectly. This was an extremely important hardware test, for the Shuttle could not land with her bay doors open. The balance of the mission saw the astronauts facing minor problems with on-board equipment, but all were just "glitches" that never endangered the crew or the mission itself. In short, the first flight of the STS hardware went extremely well.

Re-entry procedures for *Columbia* began in the 36th orbit, just 53 hours into the mission. The OMS (Orbital Maneuvering Subsystem) engines began the re-entry procedures as *Columbia* flew over the Indian Ocean. Young and Crippen then positioned *Columbia* in a nose-first attitude using the RCS (Reaction Control System). Entry interface (the first significant traces of the earth's atmosphere) occurred at an altitude of about 400,000 feet at a speed of Mach 25. *Columbia* crossed the United States coastline at about 150,000 feet of altitude and a much slower Mach 6. As *Columbia* continued her descent, Bob Crippen was heard to say "What a way to come to California." The ship touched down on the dry lake bed at Edwards Air Force Base in California on April 14 as NASA and the American public exulted at a very successful first flight.

Keeping with tradition, the official patch for STS-1 is described as a 4" emblem. Its shape is quite unusual, resembling a keyhole. The background of the patch is a circle, formed by the earth. A triangular vector is superimposed over the globe. Both the vector and the earth are surrounded by an elliptical orbital path trailing from the *Columbia*. Because of its unusual shape, STS-1 is a hand-cut emblem with an embroidered border. The border color is white.

The earth is depicted in shades of white and blue, with no land mass detailed. The vector has a navy background surrounding a topside view of the *Columbia*. It is mounted on the ET and SRB's and trails rocket blasts of red and yellow. The Orbiter, External Tank, and Solid Rocket Boosters are all sewn in white, with black added for detail. The left delta wing of the Shuttle is decorated with an American flag. The orbital aspect of the flight is symbolized by a second depiction of *Columbia* orbiting the earth. The Orbiter is sewn in a side-view trailing a red ellipse around the globe. The two views of the Shuttle are meant to emphasize the aspects of the first flight and the orbital capability. The crew's surnames are sewn in white at the bottom of the patch. Just above them, the name *Columbia* is sewn in navy blue, matching the background of the launch vector.

A 3" souvenir version of the patch closely resembles the official one. The major differences (other than size) can be seen in the way the colors are embroidered into the patch. A greater portion of this emblem is sewn with white and red. Areas containing blue and yellow are not as big, proportionately, as they are in the official version. In addition, the stitching is larger and spaced more loosely, thereby using less material. This is normal, since the main function of the souvenir patches are to provide a less expensive version of the emblem. Fewer colors and looser stitching mean lower costs for production and, therefore, a lower retail price.

Columbia became the first spacecraft to make a second flight on November 12, 1981, when Joe Engle (Commander) and Richard Truly (Pilot) took her into earth orbit. There had been four delays in relaunching *Columbia*, stretching out for two months past the first scheduled date. The most serious problem was the result of a fuel spill on the *Columbia*'s nose during a fueling procedure. The spilled liquid (nitrogen tetroxide) soaked through the heat shield tiles, destroying their adhesive and penetrating the thermal blankets. As a result, several hundred tiles and a number of thermal blankets had to be replaced. This problem alone caused a delay of one month. Another launch attempt was scrubbed when on-board computers halted countdown with 31 seconds left to launch. After an eight-day delay, another attempt was made. Launch was finally accomplished after a two-hour delay caused by persistent, minor technical problems. NASA decided to cut the flight to a "minimum mission" of less than 50% of the planned duration.

Columbia's second lift-off went smoothly, but trouble began to develop a little after 8 minutes into the flight. Flight speed at Main Engine Cut-Off (MECO) was 25,668 ft/sec which was only 1 ft/sec below nominal. One of the three Auxiliary Power Units (APU) was malfunctioning and one of the three fuel cells began to overload with water. It was decided several hours later that fuel cell # 1 would have to be shut down for the duration of the mission.

With one-third of its power lost, STS-2's mission objectives were in jeopardy. There was discussion about not activating one of the main payloads, the OSTA-1 (acronym for the Office of Space and Terrestrial Applications, now known as the Office of Space Science and Applications) experiment package, for fear that it would drain an excessive amount of power from the two remaining batteries. Eventually, it was decided to risk powering up the experiment package. To everyone's relief OSTA-1's power use had no significant effect on other Shuttle operations.

NASA officially announced the minimum mission decision on the second day of the flight. The Remote Manipulator Arm (RMS) was deployed for the first time, in spite of the shortened mission, since testing it was a major objective. On earth, astronaut Sally Ride acted as capcom for the RMS activities, making her the first woman capcom in NASA's history. Four hours of RMS work were accomplished without mishap. The worst problem that occurred, near the end of the test, was the failure of the two television cameras attached to the "wrist" and "elbow" of the RMS. OSTA scientists had planned and simulated a 54-hour mission, which meant that the only major data loss in their package resulted from the inability to observe ground targets at specific times. OSTA's synthetic-aperture radar exposed all of its film, ocean-color data was obtained, and all primary geographical targets on earth were located and examined.

Re-entry also provided several problems, although none of a major or life-threatening nature. As the astronauts entered communication blackout prior to landing, they were instructed to prepare for a manual landing. When they emerged from blackout some 16 minutes later, they were surprised at receiving new instructions to switch runways and make an autoland. However, this was another systems' test that needed to be performed. Weather conditions were such that the decision to go "auto" was made at the last possible moment. Touchdown was right on the runway centerline, and accomplished without trouble. Nine days after landing at Edwards, *Columbia* returned to Kennedy Space Center and was redesignated STS-3.

The official emblem for STS-2 is essentially round. It is a fully embroidered 4" patch and has an embroidered border of silver mylar. The *Columbia* is depicted at the right side of the emblem. Her nose extends just beyond the edge of the patch, as if she is leaping skyward. Trailing behind the Orbiter is a merged American flag and an American bald eagle. The flag is symbolic of the United States, as is the eagle. In keeping with the patriotic theme, the colors of the patch are predominantly red, white and blue.

The stars and stripes of the flag are the traditional red and white. One can also see the familiar blue field with its white stars. The body of the eagle is embroidered in white, as is his head. Detail is added with black thread. The eagle's beak and eye are sewn with gold. The astronauts' surnames are embroidered in black in the eagle's body just above the flag. Columbia is sewn in white against a navy background just above the eagle's head. At the upper right, two bright stars illuminate the sky. These two stars represent not only the two crewmen; but the second Shuttle mission, as well. They are also symbols to remind us that this was the second flight of the *Columbia*; the first time that a spaceship was able to make more than one space flight.

A 3" souvenir version of the emblem is also fully embroidered. It has the same silver mylar border, and is accurate in duplicating the colors of the official emblem. The astronauts' names are difficult to read since they are single stitched. This type of stitching is caused by the smaller size of the emblem.

In addition to the 3" version, there are at least two other souvenir "knock-offs" of the STS-2 official patch. Both of them can be considered 4" emblems. One is fully embroidered and has an embroidered border, just like the one of the official patch. However, the border is sewn with silver as opposed to silver mylar. In addition, the upper background is embroidered in the same royal blue as the field of the American flag. In the official version this background is navy blue. The detail work on the eagle is also sewn in royal blue. Finally, the two stars were sewn with the same silver thread that forms the border.

The second 4" souvenir emblem differs from the official in a more dramatic fashion. First, the border of this emblem is a ravel-proof overlock style rather than an embroidered one. In addition, it is made in royal blue. The patch is not fully embroidered either. The blue field of the American flag, and the blue background of the patch are formed by navy twill material. As a result, neither of these two emblems quite matches the beauty of the official version. However, it is quite easy to differentiate them from the official version at a glance.

STS-3 was the third mission of the shuttle series as well as the third flight of the Orbiter *Columbia*. Columbia lifted off on March 22, 1982, to begin her third journey into space. The crew were Commander Jack Lousma, a veteran of Skylab, and Pilot Gordon Fullerton, who was making his first space flight (although he was a prime crew member on the *Enterprise* ALT tests). The launch procedure went well. The only problem was a failed heater on a nitrogen-gas purge line. This caused a short delay for launch, but was quickly remedied.

Across the country at Edwards Air Force Base, things were not proceeding as smoothly. Heavy rainstorms were flooding the dry lake bed and turning the shuttle landing site into a quagmire of mud. Trainloads of equipment and personnel were hurriedly dispatched to Northrup, White Sands, New Mexico. The gypsum-sand landing strips at White Sands were the substitute of preference for the dry-lake bed at Dryden.

Soon after becoming weightless, Lousma suffered from nausea and vomiting, just as he did on Skylab 3. Fullerton was also affected by space-sickness the first three days of the flight. There were no major equipment problems although minor ones did continue to crop up. The most serious was a failure in the S-band receiver-transmitter communications system. There were also problems with the toilet (which had not functioned properly on the first two missions either), and the thermostat that controlled the cabin temperature.

Perhaps the most significant achievement of STS-3 was the first removal and retrieval of a payload by the Remote Manipulator System (RMS) or Shuttle Arm. The RMS had been built by Spar Aerospace, a Canadian firm, and was that country's contribution to the Shuttle hardware. Fullerton grasped the Plasma Diagnostics Package with the RMS, lifted it from the cargo bay, and swung it out into space. He was able to return it to the bay later without problem or mishap. This meant that the Shuttle could effectively perform one of its main design functions by launching and retrieving satellite and experiment packages on future missions.

The astronauts prepared to land on March 29, but were given a 24-hour "wave-off" only 39 minutes before the scheduled landing due to high winds at the White Sands landing strip. Preparations began for a landing on the concrete runway at Cape Kennedy in the event that weather conditions in New Mexico did not improve. The landing strip at Dryden was still too wet. However, conditions at White Sands did improve and STS-3 was able to land there the following day. It is the only Shuttle mission to date that has not landed at either Dryden or Kennedy Space Center, the two primary landing sites. One week after landing in New Mexico, *Columbia* was once again back at Cape Kennedy, being refitted for her journey as mission STS-4.

The patch for STS-3 was designed by space artist Robert C. McCall of Paradise Valley, Arizona, and depicts the Orbiter flying towards the viewer directly out of a stylized sun. The spacescape is encompassed by a navy-blue sphere representing deep space. The official emblem has a 4″ diameter and is fully embroidered. The border is embroidered in light blue.

The sun is embroidered in yellow and orange thread. Three prominent rays extend to the top and the lower sides of the patch. They are representative of the mission designation, STS-3. The surnames of the astronauts are embroidered in light blue thread to match the border and flank the Orbiter at the top of the patch. The name *Columbia* is embroidered in white thread.

The *Columbia*'s cargo-bay doors are open, and the RMS is extended with a payload package in its grasp, symbolizing one of the main objectives of the mission (i.e., testing the RMS ability to deploy future payloads). The Orbiter is sewn in white, with light blue and black added for detail. Lousma and Fullerton also commissioned a limited quantity of 5″ patches in this design for their personal use. These patches were given to close friends and family and have never been available to the general public. They do, however, duplicate the official design exactly.

The souvenir version of STS-3 is, like most, a 3″ emblem. It is remarkably true to the official design, differing from it in only two other ways. First, although the border color is the same as that of the official patch it is a ravel-proof overlock style. The second change is made in the background of the patch. Again, the color is true to the official version, but this emblem has a twill background rather than an embroidered one. The detail achieved in the depiction of the Orbiter is remarkable, and nearly as intricate as the 4″. This patch certainly does belong to anyone's collection of Space or Shuttle patches.

STS-4 was the final mission of the "test-flight" phase of the Shuttle Program. *Columbia* was the mission spacecraft for the fourth time. She was crewed by Ken Mattingly (Commander) and Henry Hartsfield (Pilot). *Columbia* achieved an on-time lift-off, the first mission to do so, on June 27, 1982. STS-4 was also the first Shuttle mission to carry a Department of Defense (DOD) payload: the Cryogenic Infra-red Radiance Telescope (Cirris). Cirris is designed to identify Soviet missiles and aircraft against earth's background.

STS-4 also carried the first payload belonging to a commercial concern (McDonnell Douglas Astronautics Co.), the Continuous Flow Electrophoresis System (CFES), which separates biological materials in a fluid according to their surface electrical charge. These "pure" materials can then be used in the manufacture of advanced medicines for use on earth. CFES experiments continue to be flown on Shuttle missions, as they have proven that some materials can be manufactured in a gravity-free environment much better than on earth.

Firsts for STS-4 also included the first operational "Get Away Special" experiment canister to be carried on a Shuttle mission. Getaway Specials (officially titled Small Self-Contained Payloads) are an ongoing program of science experiments which are flown on Shuttle missions on a space-available basis. "Get Away Specials" are available to industry, educational organizations, and domestic and foreign governments for legitimate scientific purposes. Anyone who wishes to may fly a small experiment aboard the Space Shuttle. Application must be made to, and approved by, NASA. STS-4 carried nine such experiments provided by students from Utah State University.

STS-4's (and *Columbia*'s) performance was the most trouble-free of the first four flights. All problems encountered were minor, and only totalled 16. The first three flights logged 61, 50, and 47 problems, respectively. Re-entry went smoothly, and *Columbia* landed at NASA's Dryden facility at Edwards Air Force Base without trouble. For the first time, *Columbia* landed on a concrete runway rather than the dry lake bed. This enabled NASA scientists to evaluate landing performance in preparation for planned landing sequences at Kennedy Space Center on future missions. President Reagan was on hand to view the landing and watch the Orbiter *Challenger* depart (piggyback on the 747 carrier) for Cape Kennedy, where it would be readied for its first flight into space.

The official patch for STS-4 is oval-shaped. It is a 4" emblem (measured across the widest part of the oval). Most collectors agree that STS-4 is, unfortunately, the least attractive patch in the Shuttle series. In fact, souvenir versions of the emblem are much more attractive. The official patch is sewn with a red embroidered border and a fully embroidered interior. The red border is so narrow that the patch has somewhat of an unfinished look. Most souvenir versions have ravel-proof overlock borders which seem to give the design a cleaner, more finished appearance.

The background of the official patch is sewn in three shades of light blue. The *Columbia* is depicted trailing our nation's colors in a ribbon extending from a light-blue earth. The ribbon forms a "4" denoting the mission designation of this flight. It also creates the impression that *Columbia* is streaking away from earth into the future. To emphasize this symbolism, the Orbiter's nose extends just beyond the edge of the patch on the right-hand side. The future, in this case, is meant to be the operational phase of the Shuttle program, which began with mission STS-5. The reader will remember that STS-4 was the last of the flight-test missions for the Shuttle hardware.

The surnames of the crew, Mattingly and Hartsfield, are embroidered in white just below the Orbiter and the tri-colored ribbon. Columbia is also embroidered in large white letters just above the earth, and running along one side of the 4.

There are two excellent souvenir versions of the STS-4 emblem. The first is the same size as the official patch. It is not fully embroidered; rather, a light-blue twill was used to create the majority of the patch background. Like the official patch, it depicts the Orbiter extending just beyond the edge of the oval, trailing a red, white and blue ribbon. The thread colors of this version are quite close to those of the official patch, as well. Close observation will reveal some color differences in the earth and the outer background, but these are minor. The overall look of the patch is enhanced by a ravel-proof overlock border sewn in red.

The second souvenir version of STS-4 is a large emblem. In fact, it is larger in size than the official emblem. It measures 5" across the widest portion of the oval and 3" at the height. It is a fully embroidered patch with very crisp, tight embroidery. The blue background is somewhat darker than that of the official patch, but overall the colors match the NASA version quite well. Like the smaller souvenir patch, this large version has a red, ravel-proof, overlock border.

STS-5, the fifth Shuttle mission, included many firsts. Most important, it was the first operational Shuttle flight. It was also the first Shuttle flight to launch a commercial satellite. Other firsts included: the first four-man crew in outer space; the first mission specialists—Dr. William Lenoir and Dr. Joe Allen—and the first photographs taken from the Shuttle during landing operations. STS-5 had to forego another first—the first EVA demonstrating the new Extra-vehicular Mobility Units (EMUs)—when they failed to operate properly. NASA officials were extremely disappointed by this as the EVA was to be one of the major accomplishments of the mission.

STS-5 launched from Cape Kennedy on November 11, 1982. *Columbia*'s fifth countdown and launch went so smoothly that lift-off occurred only .0678 seconds behind schedule. In addition to the two mission specialists, *Columbia*'s crew included Vance Brand (Commander) and Robert Overmyer (Pilot). Parking orbit was achieved after two OMS burns some two hours into the flight with no major problems. As *Columbia* completed her third orbit she passed below the Soviet's Salyut 7 space station. The two crews were unable to communicate with each other, but the crew of Salyut 7 must have been able to monitor *Columbia*'s passage with her sensors.

Two commercial satellites were launched from the cargo bay of STS-5. The first was Satellite Business System's SBS-3, which was designed to provide all-digital communications and features time-division, multiple-access techniques for efficient use of satellite transmission communications. This means that SBS-3 could provide high capacity private networks for voice, data, video and electronic mail transmission across the entire United States.

The second satellite, Canada's Anik C-3, was launched on the second day of the mission. Anik C-3 was the fifth satellite in the Anik series, but the first launched by the Space Shuttle. Anik C-3 became part of the Telesat Canada network which provides voice, message, data, facsimile and broadcast service to remote and northern parts of Canada. Anik C-3 was the first in the series to provide rooftop-to-rooftop transmissions which were and are especially important to Canadian businesses (particularly Canadian pay-TV and other broadcast services).

STS-5 carried three student experiments which were selected from proposals made by students from all across the United States. These proposals were encouraged and developed under a program supervised by NASA and the National Science Teachers Association. In addition, the mission carried a Get Away Special canister, which contained an experiment from the material science program of the German Ministry of Research and Technology.

The plan for an EVA was abandoned when Allen and Lenoir could not overcome malfunctions in their spacesuits. This meant that tests of tools for construction of space stations could not be carried out, nor could the astronauts attempt a training exercise aimed at developing emergency manual procedures for closing the payload doors. STS-5 landed at Edwards with Commander Vance Brand flying a fully manual landing from Mach .97 to touchdown. The roll-out at landing went very smoothly, although the inboard wheel on the main landing gear locked during the landing and shredded the tire. Since this could have caused major handling problems, it did cause concern among NASA personnel. The entire assembly was later examined to determine the reasons for the lock-up, so the problem could be prevented on future flights.

During and after the mission there was also a great deal of concern expressed about the high rate of spacesickness experienced by the astronauts. The Air Force was particularly concerned since DOD payloads must be off-loaded early in a mission (often as early as the first or second orbit), and spacesickness could limit an astronaut's ability to perform the necessary tasks to accomplish this. NASA stated publicly that the spacesickness was no worse than that encountered by many sailors, and, indeed, the astronauts themselves (worried, no doubt, about their prospects for future flights) protested that there had been too much public discussion of the problem. Nevertheless, a few weeks after the mission, NASA announced a program to study the cause and prevention of spacesickness. An extra astronaut was added to the crew of upcoming missions STS-7 and STS-8 specifically to begin studies.

If the official patch for STS-4 can be said to be one of the least attractive in the Shuttle series, then the emblem for STS-5 is nearly its exact opposite. The official version of the STS-5 patch is a 4" diameter, round emblem. It has a ravel-proof, overlock border sewn in yellow gold. As is normal, the patch is fully embroidered. A wide inner band of brilliant red contains the two astronauts' and two mission specialists' surnames sewn in royal blue. At the bottom, sewn in yellow gold, is the Orbiter name, *Columbia*. The inside of the red band is outlined with a thin band of white, separating it from the interior spacescape.

The interior scene has a navy-blue background depicting the depths of deep space. Interspersed throughout this scene are numerous stars of varying intensity, embroidered in light blue. In the foreground, *Columbia* is presented in a side view against the backdrop of a large five-pointed star. This star is also embroidered in light blue. Its five points symbolize the mission designation (STS-5). The *Columbia* is sewn in white thread, with black added for detail. Light blue is used in the shuttle for shading and aesthetic presentation. The payload doors are open, showing the satellite cradles and other details of the payload bay. Above the Shuttle the two satellites, SBS-3 and Anik C-3, are depicted powering into their final working orbits. Each satellite trails a rocket blast from the Shuttle Payload Assist Module (PAM-D) as it flies upwards from the payload bay. One satellite is slightly above the other, suggesting the time interval between their actual deployment.

The souvenir patch for STS-5 does a credible job of duplicating the official design. It does differ in that the center background is navy twill rather than Swiss embroidery. In addition, the background of the 3" patch has many fewer stars. All of these stars are of the same intensity, unlike the official patch. This lessens the impression that one is gazing into the far reaches of outer space. Detail on the shuttle and the two satellites is quite good, although the light-blue shading on the Orbiter is eliminated in this version. The border and inner band colors are well matched to the official design, and create the overall impression very well. Without scrutiny, this patch gives an extremely good impression of the official patch. It is highly recommended as a fine addition to a patch collection.

STS-6 was the first flight of the second Orbiter

in the Shuttle series, the *Challenger*. *Challenger* would fly nine successful missions, performing a wide variety of tasks. It was destroyed by an explosion 72 seconds into its tenth mission (STS-51L). Launch was achieved on April 5, 1983, after seven postponements due to such problems as engine cracks, fuel leaks and storm contamination of the satellite payload. The crew included Commander Paul Weitz, Pilot Karol Bobko, Mission Specialist Donald Peterson, and Mission Specialist Dr. Story Musgrave. NASA nicknamed this group the "Geritol crew" since their average age was 47. Commander Weitz was the oldest at 50, followed by Peterson and Musgrave, both 47, and Bobko at 45 years of age.

Challenger carried a large telecommunications satellite as its first major payload. This was the Tracking and Data Relay Satellite (TDRS-A; known more commonly by its acronym, which is pronounced as TID RUS). This was the first of three TDRS satellites planned for a telecommunication system. The TDRS system is designed to support the Space Shuttle itself, as well as scientific experiments on board and up to 26 user satellites simultaneously. This would eliminate the need for the network of costly ground stations worldwide, for TDRS would allow multiple-access service from a number of satellites, relaying information to the ground. TDRS also provides a single-access service which allows two high data-rate communication relays. The TDRS satellites do not process data in either direction (to or from satellites in space), but rather operate as "bent-pipe" repeaters; relaying signals and data between a user spacecraft and a ground terminal. For the Space Shuttle, this meant that communications with ground stations could occur for nearly all of its orbital period once the TDRS system was in place. Prior to TDRS, communication between the Shuttle and the ground-station network was possible for only about 15% (typically) of its orbital period.

The TDRS was deployed from the payload bay early in the mission without mishap. However, trouble soon began for the large satellite. It was to be powered into geosynchronous orbit by a device called the Inertial Upper Stage (IUS) which had been developed by the Air Force. The IUS was, in essence, a mini-rocket motor designed to boost the TDRS to its proper orbit. The first IUS stage put TDRS into its proper transfer orbit with no trouble. However, the second engine burn, designed to lift the satellite to final-orbit status, failed to work properly. Instead it caused the TDRS to begin tumbling. At first, it was thought that the satellite was lost, but teamwork by all three ground-control centers was finally successful in bringing the satellite somewhat under control. The tumbling was stopped and its solar panels were extended in time to save its depleted batteries. Over a period of several weeks following the mission, the TDRS was eventually maneuvered into its proper orbit.

STS-6 would also include as another major event, the EVA that had to be scrubbed from the STS-5 mission. The two mission specialists, Peterson and Musgrave, spent just over four hours "walking" and working in the payload bay. The two mission specialists attached themselves to the sides of the bay with tethers and tried out various work stations, practiced using assorted tools, and demonstrated suit mobility. They were also able to winch the payload bay doors closed, proving that this could be done manually should an emergency ever require it.

After five days in space, *Challenger* ended its first mission successfully with a center-line landing on Edwards's runway #22. NASA's second Orbiter had performed well on its first mission. NASA could relish the accomplishments of its growing fleet, and continue to strive for more. The Shuttle System was proving itself to be generally dependable and reliable despite its glitches.

The STS-6 flight is symbolized by the hexagonal shape of its patch. The official patch is a 4", fully embroidered emblem. The overall color theme of the patch is a patriotic red, white and blue. It has a ravel-proof overlock border of royal blue, which surrounds an inner band of white. This inner band is bordered on the interior by a thin red line. As usual, this band contains the surnames of the crew and mission designation. *Challenger* is embroidered in red at the top of the patch. At the bottom is the mission designation, STS-6, also in red. The surnames of the crew are embroidered in royal blue to match the border. The two astronauts' names are sewn in the upper sides; Weitz to the left, and Bobko to the right. The mission specialists' names are located on the lower sides of the hexagon; Peterson on the left, and Musgrave on the right.

The center area of the patch is dominated by a

spacescape, which depicts the Orbiter flying by in the foreground as it creates an orbital path from behind the earth. The planet is depicted as a large, light-blue sphere, rimmed with a slightly darker blue. The Orbiter is seen in a side (and slightly frontal) view with the payload bay doors open. The TDRS, combined with the IUS, can be seen above the payload doors. It trails a white streamer behind the far side of the globe, just as the *Challenger* trails a red one. Both the Orbiter and the TDRS are sewn in shades of white, with light blue shading and black detail. The IUS is also sewn with a band of red.

Slightly above and behind *Challenger* are six stars which form the constellation Virgo. These six stars are representative of the flight designation. Virgo itself is also symbolic of the maiden flight of the Shuttle *Challenger*. These stars are sewn in white against an embroidered background of deep navy, which represents the depths of space.

A 3″ souvenir version of the patch duplicates the design and color of the official version very well. Its lettering is a bit crowded due to the size of the emblem, but is otherwise excellent in its execution. Like the official version it is hexagonal in shape and has a royal-blue, ravel-proof overlock border. A slightly larger 3½″ souvenir version is not quite as accurate a representation. In the larger depiction, the patch has a navy-blue border. In addition, the reds of the lettering and design detail are really more of an orange shade than a true NASA red. In addition, the crew's names are sewn in a lighter shade of blue than the royal color used in the official and the 3″ version.

It is interesting to collectors to note the differences between the various souvenir patches and the official ones. As has been noted before, there are many reasons they can differ from the official emblem. Often, the primary reason for reducing the size is to lower the eventual retail-price structure. This is also the case quite often for reducing the number of thread colors that is sewn into the patch. When a different color is used (as in the case of the 3½″ STS-6 patch just discussed), it is often the result of artistic interpretation by the manufacturer, or the reliance upon an early version of the patch design. In the case of the 3½″ STS-6 emblem, the differences in color appear to be ones of interpretation.

The seventh flight in the Space Shuttle Program was the second flight for the Orbiter *Challenger*. The crew consisted of two astronauts and three mission specialists, making it the largest single-mission crew in the history of the American space program. Included were Commander Bob Crippen, the first person to make two Shuttle flights; Pilot Frederick Hauck; Lead Mission Specialist John Fabian; Mission Specialist Dr. Norman Thagard; and Mission Specialist Dr. Sally Ride, the first American woman and the youngest astronaut to fly a space mission. Thagard was not originally a member of the STS-7 crew, but was added in December of 1982 (after the spacesickness problems of STS-5) to conduct medical tests and collect data on several physiological changes that are associated with astronauts' adaptation to a space environment.

The prime pre-flight objectives for the mission were to deploy two commercial communications satellites and perform the first landing on the three-mile long runway at NASA's Kennedy Space Center. Unfortunately, the landing at Kennedy had to be scrubbed due to inclement weather. Instead, STS-7 landed at NASA's Dryden facility at Edwards Air Force Base, as had all but one mission before it.

The two commercial satellites carried on STS-7 were Telesat Canada's Anik C and Indonesia's Palapa B communications satellites. Anik C was the second Anik series satellite deployed by the Shuttle (the first had been placed in orbit on STS-5), and was released on the first day of the mission. Palapa B was deployed on the second day of the mission. Its purpose was to provide voice, video, telephone and high-speed data services which would electronically link Indonesia's many islands and bring advanced tele communications to that nation's 130 million inhabitants.

STS-7 also carried the Shuttle Pallet Satellite (SPAS); a space platform that could operate inside or outside the payload bay. The SPAS was deployed and recaptured by Mission Specialist Dr. Sally Ride, who used the RMS "arm" of the Shuttle.

The cargo bay also carried the first U.S./German cooperative materials science payload, which was called OSTA-2. This acronym means Office of Space and Terrestrial Applications (a branch of NASA). It is now known as the Office of Space Science and Applications.

The McDonnell Douglas CFES electrophoresis experiment also flew in the Orbiter's mid-deck along with seven Getaway Special payloads. The CFES results were so successful that they led to a decision to fly the first commercial (ie, private non-NASA) industrial payload specialist. Charles Walker, of McDonnell Douglas, was named as a crew member of the upcoming STS-41D mission, in order to operate a prototype production unit continuously throughout the flight.

The official emblem for the STS-7 mission is a round, 4" diameter patch. It has an outer band of red circled by a ravel-proof overlock border of a matching shade. At the top of the band, *Challenger* is sewn in white thread. At the bottom, the crew members' surnames are also sewn in white. A thin white line borders the outer band and frames the inner space scene.

The inner scene has a fully embroidered background of navy blue which, as it often does, represents the background of outer space. Dispersed throughout this background are seven bright white stars which symbolize the mission designation, STS-7. At the right, a bright yellow sun shines on the earth and underside of the Orbiter. Joined in the center of the sun are five white symbols: four for the males and one for the female. They represent the five crew members—four men and one woman, who flew STS-7.

A head-on view of the Orbiter dominates the center of the scene as it orbits the blue-white globe below. The lower side of *Challenger* is highlighted with gold, as if reflecting the sun. The payload doors are open, and the RMS is extended in the shape of an Arabic 7. This is an additional symbol of the mission designation. The Orbiter is sewn primarily with white thread. Silver and grey are used for aesthetic shading and black is added for detail. Like most of the official emblems in the Shuttle series, STS-7 is a fully embroidered emblem.

The most common souvenir version of the STS-7 patch is a 3" diameter emblem. Unlike the official patch it has a navy-blue twill background in its center. The Orbiter is not as detailed as in the 4" size, but an adequate representation is made. The symbols for the crew at the center of the sun are sewn in brown; rather than the white of the official version. In addition, the darker blues of the earth's surface, which are visible in the 4" emblem, disappear in this version. This is most probably a production-cost compromise (as is the twill background).

STS-7 is one of the most popular and collectible patches in the Shuttle series. While this may be partly ascribed to its stunning design, it is also quite likely that the popularity of America's first woman astronaut adds to its appeal. It is an excellent patch to begin a collection of Shuttle emblems since it does relate to a major "first" in the U.S. space program. Dr. Ride downplays this aspect of her role in STS-7, regarding herself as "just another member of the crew." It is no accident, however, that she is one of the most sought-after astronauts for speaking engagements and public affairs.

The main payload for Shuttle mission STS-8 was the Indian National Satellite, INSAT-1B. Because INSAT-1B had to be deployed in a particular geosynchronous orbit, STS-8 had to be, and was, the first Shuttle flight to launch at night. The flight lasted for six days, and resulted in a smooth landing at Edwards Air Force Base (which also occurred at night for the first time). *Challenger*'s third mission carried a crew of five. The Flight Commander was the U.S. Navy's Dick Truly, making his second (and last since he became Commander of the Navy's Space Command) shuttle flight; Pilot Daniel Brandenstein; Mission Specialist 1 Dale Gardner; Mission Specialist 2 Dr. Guion Bluford, who had the distinction of being America's first black astronaut, and Mission Specialist 3 Dr. William Thornton. Dr. Thornton was 54 years old at launch, which made him the world's *oldest* (perhaps a dubious distinction) astronaut to date.

INSAT-1B was deployed on orbit 17 almost exactly on its orbital target. A PAM-D carried it into its proper orbit, and though its solar panels refused to open initially, the problem was eventually solved by "rolling" the satellite's panel hinges towards the sun, allowing them to thaw. The only other cargo in STS-8's payload bay were some 260,000 stamped "Event" Covers (Envelopes). NASA hoped to recoup part of STS-8's launch expenses by selling these to collectors after the mission.

Astronauts Bluford and Gardner ran very successful electrophoresis tests throughout the flight. These included the separation of beta cells (using pancreas cells taken from live dogs), which produce insulin in the body. This is difficult to do under earth conditions. The success of these experiments on STS-8 have raised hopes that space-processed cells may restore diabetics to normal health with only one implantation.

In addition, STS-8 made a number of earth geological observations which were said to be the most detailed since those of Skylab. Because it was launched at night, STS-8 had the benefit of many hours of daylight over the Southern hemisphere. This enabled the crew to observe features of southern Africa and central Australia, as well as many active volcanoes and ocean currents in the Pacific. Much work was also done using the TDRS-1 for communication links. TDRS performed well, providing better TV and voice communication than had previously been experienced from space. Testing the TDRS successfully was particularly important since its communication ability would play a key role in the next mission, STS-9, and its payload Spacelab I.

The official patch for the STS-8 depicts the night launch of the Orbiter *Challenger*'s third mission. It is a 4" diameter, round emblem with a red, ravel-proof, overlock border. The border is broken at the top by the fuel tank of the Shuttle as it rockets into space. A white band encircles the inner scene, containing the surnames of the five crew members embroidered in red.

The spacescape at the center of the patch is particularly striking. At the bottom, the earth can be seen falling into the distance, as the Shuttle powers into space. The Orbiter's main engines flash blue flame, tinged with white. At the same time, the SRB's trail yellow and orange flames as they begin to separate from the Orbiter. The entire configuration flys upside down from an earthly point of view, just as it does in an actual launch mode. Above the Orbiter, the bronze-toned ET will soon separate from the spacecraft and begin its fiery descent into the earth's atmosphere.

In the foreground of the scene, *Challenger* is sewn in silver mylar, denoting the mission vehicle. The part of the earth which is visible is a blue-white sphere, tinged with gold and yellow at the horizon, symbolic of the night launch and the coming sunrise. The sky behind *Challenger* is a dark navy blue, devoid of detail, save for eight silver stars. These eight stars are of the constellation Aquila, "The Eagle," and symbolize the mission designation (STS-8).

A 3" souvenir interpretation of the STS-8 emblem is also a popular collectible. Unlike the official patch, the ET does not extend beyond the border in this version. In addition, the navy background is twill, not fully embroidered, as in the official emblem. The patch is simplified further by using fewer colors in the ET, the earth and the flames of the space vehicles. It must be noted, however, that even the souvenir version of STS-8 is quite striking. The design of this emblem makes it one of the most beautiful (and collectible) in the Shuttle series. We highly recommend both versions to space-patch collectors.

STS-8 also had a second patch which symbolized a certain aspect of the flight. Commander Richard Truly was the only "veteran" flying on STS-8 (he was making his second Shuttle flight). The other four crew members were all "rookies" making their first flight. In a humorous play on this situation, the STS-8 crew patch was conceived. The patch is not official, but was made for the crew as a joke. It is a round, 4" diameter emblem, sewn in two colors (black and white).

The black background (twill) is meant to suggest the night launch aspect of the flight. The crew's surnames are sewn at the top of the patch, with the mission designation and the Orbiter name embroidered at the bottom. In the center of the patch, two "windshields" of the Shuttle can be seen. On the right-hand side, Commander Truly (wearing spectacles), or rather, his eyes, can be seen gazing casually out the window at the scene ahead. The eyes are depicted somewhat heavy-lidded, or perhaps almost bored. Remember that Truly was the veteran making his second flight. The wonders of space flight might seem routine to him. At the left, four pairs of wide-open, rounded eyes can be seen peering out. They seem a bit awed, perhaps even a bit nervous, as they make their first journey into space. Thus are Brandenstein, Gardner, Bluford, and Thornton depicted in the crew patch of STS-8.

Since the crew patch was not an official Shuttle emblem, it was made in relatively small quantities. Most went to friends of the crew and workers on the mission. The patch can still be found on occasion today, although with some difficulty. Replicas have been produced by one or more emblem manufacturers and will sometimes appear in a catalog or retail outlet. Probably the best bet to obtain one, however, is from another collector.

STS-9, the ninth flight in the Shuttle series, was a ten-day flight that began on November 28, 1983. The main cargo of STS-9 was Spacelab 1, the first flight of the European Space Agency's orbital laboratory. The mission was a cooperative endeavor of NASA and ESA, and included the first non-American to fly in a U.S. spacecraft, Dr. Ulf Merbold, of West Germany. Five Americans accompanied Merbold on this flight, thereby becoming the largest crew to have ever flown in one spacecraft. Commander of the flight was John Young, making a historic sixth flight into space. The Pilot was Brewster Shaw (making his first flight). Mission Specialist 1 was Dr. Owen Garriott, a veteran of Skylab 2, making his second flight. Mission Specialist 2 was Dr. Robert Parker. Dr. Byron Lichtenberg, the final member of the crew, joined Dr. Merbold as the first two Payload Specialists to fly in the Shuttle. Payload Specialists are career scientists and engineers—men and women—selected by their peers to fly in space on a particular mission and devote themselves to conducting experiments. They are not trained to fly the Shuttle or operate its systems.

STS-9 was the maiden flight of Spacelab, which had been developed by the European Space Agency (ESA). It was flown by the Orbiter *Columbia*, which had been outfitted especially for Spacelab. The flight of STS-9 was a landmark of international cooperation for space research. It was also the first American space flight to carry career scientists from outside NASA's astronaut corps. Spacelab was designed, developed, funded and built by ESA as Europe's contribution to the United States Space Transportation System. It represents a European investment in the Shuttle program that was in excess of $1 billion.

The goals for the first Spacelab mission were designed primarily to test capability. Five broad areas of research investigation were explored: life science, atmospheric physics and earth observation, astronomy and solar physics, space plasma physics, and materials science and technology.

Experiments for the mission were provided on a joint basis by 11 European countries, the United States, Canada, and Japan.

The Spacelab itself is a reusable, research laboratory facility. When installed in the Shuttle cargo bay, it converts the Orbiter into a versatile, on-orbit research center. Spacelab consists of two major elements. The first is a pressurized, habitable laboratory called a module. Scientists can work in the module in their shirtsleeves, without having to wear bulky, cumbersome spacesuits. The second element consists of unpressurized platforms called pallets, which are designed to support instruments such as telescopes, sensors and antennas which require direct exposure to space. These two elements may be used separately or in various combinations, returned to earth, and reused on subsequent flights.

The Spacelab module comes in two sections: a core segment and an experiment segment. The core segment houses data-processing equipment and utilities for the module and pallets when both are flown together. It also contains lab fixtures such as experiment racks, work benches and a viewport for optical experiments and photography.

The experiment segment provides further pressurized work areas, space for additional experiment racks, and provisions for mounting either the window assembly or a scientific airlock designed to enable the crew to expose experiments carried in the module to the space environment. The core segment can be flown by itself (called the short-module configuration) or coupled in tandem with the experiment segment (the long-module configuration).

The Spacelab pallets, which form the second part of the Spacelab configuration, are U-shaped frame and panel structures. As many as five Spacelab pallets can be flown in the cargo bay. These can be flown with or without the Spacelab module. When no module is flown, payload specialists operate experiments from the aft flight deck of the Shuttle Orbiter.

The crew of STS-9 provided twenty-four operation of Spacelab 1 by working in 12-hour shifts. The Red team (day crew) of Young, Parker and Merbold and the Blue team (night crew) of Shaw, Garriott and Lichtenberg staggered their meals and sleeping times so the Spacelab could function continuously. Scientists on earth were well pleased at the number of experiments the crew were able to perform.

STS-9 landed smoothly at Edwards Air Force Base after a short delay caused by computer problems. The mission was extended by five orbits while "crashing" computers were realigned and checked. The errant computer stayed on line until touchdown, when it failed again. Of course, it was hardly a problem at that point. Spacelab scientists celebrated a mission that accomplished 98% of its experimental objectives; although NASA announced that no future flights would attempt to cover so many different disciplines.

The official emblem for the STS-9 mission is a 4" shield. Like other mission patches it is fully embroidered. The patch border is red, overlock, and ravel-proof. At the bottom of the shield, a white band carries the Orbiter name, *Columbia*, and the Spacelab 1 mission designation. The balance of the perimeter is embroidered with a red band which incorporates the surnames of the crew. These are sewn in white: the Commander and Pilot at the top, the Mission and Payload Specialists' at either side.

The center spacescape is ringed by three narrow bands; one of royal blue, sandwiched between two of white. The background of the inner scene is the typical dark navy-blue color which so often symbolizes the depths of outer space. The foreground of the scene is dominated by the Orbiter flying towards the viewer with her cargo bay doors open. Inside, the Spacelab can be seen, resting on the cargo bed. The Orbiter trails a blue and white path which forms an Arabic nine. This, of course, represents the mission designation (STS-9). In the background, bits of the blue/white marble earth can be seen. No specific land masses are visible, as is often the case in flights with international participation and significance. Nine white stars complete the background, and also tell the viewer that this patch is mission nine in the Shuttle series.

STS-9 is a popular patch with collectors because of its international scope. ESA developed its own emblem for this mission, and there is also a separate Spacelab 1 patch which celebrates this flight (these are discussed in the International Patches chapter). This mission reflects an important trend for the future of space exploration. Cooperation between many nations in space endeavors will become more and more prevalent. These joint ventures will enable smaller countries to share in the technological benefits of space in ways that are not possible for them individually.

Even the United States (and NASA) is eager to share the high costs of continued space activity. In this country, and around the world, private enterprise is being encouraged to commercialize space exploration. Joint ventures between nations and governments are further examples of cost- and data-sharing. Spacelab 1 (and its patches) represents one of the first major steps in this area. For this reason, it is prized by beginner and advanced collectors alike.

The souvenir version of STS-9 differs from the official mainly in that it is smaller in size, and is not fully embroidered. It is considered to be a 3" patch, and employs a red twill material as a background, replacing the embroidered band around the upper edges of the patch. The blue coloration of the earth and the trailing nine are also darker than those of the official emblem. This patch is nicely detailed and warrants addition to any space or Shuttle patch collection.

Mission STS-10 in the Shuttle series does not exist. A flight by this designation was originally scheduled as a Department of Defense mission. Its cargo and specific mission were classified. The flight was cancelled long before its scheduled launch date because the military cargo was not operational. Thus the tenth flight in the shuttle program is known as STS-11 or STS-41B.

This second designation, STS-41B, reflects a change which occurred in NASA's flight numbering system during this time. STS is still an acronym for Shuttle Transportation System, as it has been. The second half of the mission label now imparts more information than a simple mission number sequence. The first number represents the (NASA's) fiscal year any given flight occurred. For example, 4 means fiscal 1984; 5 fiscal 1985; and so on. The second number in the sequence is indicative of the mission launch site. Kennedy Space Center is represented by 1, the site where all Shuttle flights to date, have begun.

Beginning in 1986, Shuttles are also scheduled to be launched from the west coast of the United States at Vandenberg Air Force Base in California. This will give the Shuttle the important ability to operate in polar orbits as well as the present equatorial orbital ability gained by launching from Kennedy Space Center. All launches from Vandenberg will be designated by a 2 in the second position of the mission designation. The letter at the end of the label indicates the order of a flight in any given fiscal year. That is, A would be first, B second, C third, and so on. It will be possible, for example, to have one mission labelled

71-A and another mission to be designated 72-A. Finally, a mission will keep its designation, even if it is later rescheduled in the missions' sequence.

STS-41B lifted off from Cape Canaveral on February 3, 1984. The mission had three main objectives: first, launch the Westar VI satellite from the cargo bay, followed by the second objective, successful launch of the Palapa-B2. The third objective was to provide extensive testing of the Manned Maneuvering Unit (MMU) in untethered spacewalks, essential to a later mission's rescue and repair of the disabled Solar Maximum satellite.

Mission Commander Vance Brand, making his third flight into space, was accompanied by a team of four rookies. These were Pilot Robert "Hoot" Gibson; Mission Specialist 1 Ronald McNair; Mission Specialist 2 (and EV-2) Robert Stewart; and Mission Specialist 3 (EV-1) Bruce McCandless. McCandless was making his first flight after being in the astronaut corps for nearly eighteen years. He was EV-1 on this mission because he had spent most of that time working on MMU development.

The flight caused much early disappointment with the failure of both satellites. The Westar 6 was deployed to the wrong orbit when the PAM-D upper stage failed to complete its burn. Two days later, Indonesia's Palapa B-2 suffered a similar fate with identical results. The Orbiter and the astronauts had performed their tasks without fault, but two consecutive failures of the PAM-D (heretofore completely reliable) placed an entire year of Shuttle launches in jeopardy. The fifth and seventh days of the mission raised spirits when the MMU's performed impeccably. Astronaut Bruce McCandless made space history by becoming the first human satellite. McCandless flew the untethered MMU over 300 feet from the Shuttle, completely under its own power. He spent nearly six hours on the first EVA, testing the techniques that would be needed for the rescue of the disabled Solar Maximum, an event scheduled for mission STS-41C. The versatility and performance of the MMU was stunning in its first operation. The success of this aspect of the flight helped dispel some of the disappointment over the satellite failures.

STS-41B became the first Shuttle mission to land at Kennedy Space Center. Commander Brand brought *Challenger* down on the concrete runway at Kennedy in the early morning hours, some 15 minutes after sunrise. While no alligators or bobcats wandered onto the concrete apron, feathers on the Orbiter's windshield indicated a mid-air collision during the landing. Significant damage occurred to the right main landing gear giving rise to speculation that the grooved runway at the Cape might not be a suitable surface for future landings.

The official patch for STS-41B is an oval. Its border is white and is oversewn. At the bottom, a red banner is embroidered with the surnames of the crew. At the top of the emblem, the Orbiter name, *Challenger*, is sewn in yellow gold and outlined in blue.

This mission was the fourth flight of the Orbiter *Challenger*. The space vehicle highlights and dominates the center of the patch. It is depicted in a landing mode, flying directly at the viewer. The nose of the Orbiter is angled upwards as it prepares for touchdown on the Kennedy runway. Just visible at the top are the Commander and Pilot's viewing ports.

The *Challenger* is flanked by two scenes which represent the major focus of the mission. On the left, a PAM-D assisted satellite is powered upwards into geosynchronous orbit. It is sewn in grey with red detail and black shadow. In the background, earth's horizon can be seen against the blue background of space. Six gold stars are interspersed throughout the sky. To the right of the Orbiter, a crew member (McCandless) equipped with the MMU moves freely in the space environment. Below him, the earth is depicted in light blue and white, as it is in the scene to the left. A yellow sun lies midway above the horizon, against the blue of space. In this scene, five gold stars can be seen throughout. The total number (11) of stars represent the original mission designation, STS-11. The background of the patch is embroidered completely in white. Each scene is bordered with a thin red band, matching the banner at the lower edge.

A smaller souvenir adaptation of the emblem changes the look of the patch. The smaller version has an overlock, ravel-proof border which is sewn in red. The official emblem has a white border. In addition, the white background is twill material in the smaller patch. It is fully embroidered in the official size. The color and detail of the Orbiter, satellite and astronaut are quite good in the souvenir version. The colors in the earth are the same shade as in the official emblem, as are the background shades and detail coloring. The red markings on the satellite are left out, as are the blue shading on the satellite and the MMU.

These differences do not detract from the appearance of the patch in any way. Indeed, even with a different color border, it does a remarkable job of adhering to the spirit of the official emblem. The only major mistake in the emblem has to do with the number of stars in the background of the two outer space scenes. The PAM-D scene has four stars instead of six, even though the MMU scene has the necessary five. This oversight eliminates the symbolism of the eleven stars as the mission designation.

STS-41C was launched from the Cape on April 6, 1984. Robert Crippen was making his third flight into space, and served as Commander for the mission. His Pilot was Francis "Dick" Scobee. Terry Hart was Mission Specialist 1; Dr. James van Hoften was Mission Specialist 2 and EV2; and Dr. George Nelson was Mission Specialist 3 and EV1.

This mission was dubbed the Solar Maximum Mission since its main objective was to retrieve the crippled Solar Maximum satellite. Plans called for an astronaut EVA using the MMU to rendezvous with the Solar Max, dock and stop its spinning motion. Then the RMS would be used to grasp the satellite and haul it into *Challenger*'s cargo bay. Once there, Nelson and van Hoften would act as the first "space mechanics," repairing the Solar Max, and placing it once again into its proper orbit. This was accomplished with total success over the duration of the mission.

The Solar Maximum was returned to its orbit on day 7 of the flight, working well and completely repaired. This activity gave a tremendous boost to the entire Shuttle Program, as it underscored once again the versatility and usefulness of the Orbiters. NASA and other space observers have been quick to point out that the success of STS-41C marks another milestone in mankind's ability to live and work in a permanent space environment.

Almost overshadowed by the success of the Solar Max repair was the successful deployment of the Long Duration Exposure Facility (LDEF).

LDEF is a large experiment carrier designed to carry dozens of diverse, passive experiments which can be "parked" in earth orbit for long periods of time.

The LDEF carried 57 separate experiments for this particular mission. They were organized into four major groups: material structures, power and propulsion, electronics and optics, and science. Many of these experiments were very simple, and some were (are) completely passive while orbiting in LDEF. The cylindrical pallet is scheduled to be retrieved on mission 61-I (planned for launch in September of 1986). Results of the experiments' long-term exposure to the harsh space environment will be analyzed after the facility is brought back down to earth by the Space Shuttle.

The patch for STS-41C is one of the most unusual of all space patches. It is very colorful, quite graphic, and very pretty. It is also the result of terrific design work and fascinating symbolism. The official version is 4" in diameter, and has a red, overlock, ravel-proof border.

STS-41C depicts the entire story of the mission as it is reflected in the visor of an astronaut performing an extra-vehicular activity. Careful observation will allow one to see the helmet of the space suit frame the reflective surface of the visor. The right "ear" (faceplate hinge) of the space helmet is detailed, as are the faceplate fittings and other hardware. In the upper background, a deep navy embroidery symbolizes the depths of space. The lower background is white, depicting the upper portion of the MMU when it is worn by an astronaut.

At the top of the patch, the Mission Specialists' surnames are sewn in white against the deep navy-blue background. At the bottom, a red neckband on the MMU exhibits the surnames of the Commander and the Pilot (Crippen and Scobee). The upper surface of the astronaut's faceplate reflects the edge of the earth, which is sewn in light blues and white. At the left edge of the reflection, *Challenger* extends the RMS, placing the LDEF in earth orbit. In the lower right, an astronaut performs an EVA, maneuvering the disabled Solar Maximum satellite in preparation for its retrieval and repair. The bright sun's rays are splayed throughout the reflection.

The souvenir version of the emblem creates an excellent rendering of this unusual design. It differs from the official only in its smaller size, and its twill background. The color duplication is excellent, as is the artistic detail. It is a fine addition to any collection, and deserves to be collected as much as the official version.

STS-41D was the twelfth flight in the Shuttle series, and marked the first flight of the Orbiter *Discovery*. Her crew numbered six astronauts including Commander Henry Hartsfield, Pilot Michael Coats, Mission Specialist Judith Resnik (the second American female astronaut), Mission Specialist Steven Hawley, Mission Specialist Richard Mullane, and Payload Specialist Charles Walker. Walker, an employee of McDonnell Douglas Corporation, became the first commercial payload specialist to fly in space. His job was to operate the electrophoresis experiments for his company.

Due to computer problems and an engine shutdown just 4 seconds before launch, 41-D suffered several delays in its launch schedule. As a result, 41-D was combined with 41-F, and flight 41-E was cancelled altogether. It was finally launched on August 30, 1984. This mission deployed the Solar Array, which would be needed for further development of NASA's Space Station. The Solar Array is an extendable, expandable solar-collecting device. Its purpose on the Space Station would be to provide electrical power. A collapsible version, such as the one flown on STS-41D, would be more economical and much easier to transport. 41-D provided the first space test of this technology. The Solar Array was a project directed by NASA's Office of Aeronautics and Space Technology (OAST), and the cargo has come to be called OAST-1.

The official patch of STS-41D is a 4" diameter, round emblem. It is sewn primarily in various shades of light blue. A light-blue band encircles an inner space scene and is bordered by a navy-blue overlock border. The surnames of the Commander and Pilot are sewn into the top of this band. At the sides and lower half of the patch are the surnames of the Mission Specialists in the crew.

The inner spacescape depicts a light-blue globe circled by a ribbon of red, white and blue. In the foreground, the ribbon is trailing behind the Orbiter, as a rocket blast from its engines. In the center of its length, the name *Discovery* is embroidered in red. At the end of the ribbon, a white ghost ship sails behind. The operational Shuttles were all named for famous historical sailing ships. In this patch, the ghost ship represents the Orbiter's namesakes which have figured prominently in the history of exploration. The Orbiter *Discovery* is depicted as it heads for new horizons, ready to extend that proud tradition. Against the deep-blue background of space twelve white stars shine brightly. These signify that STS-41D is the twelfth flight.

The souvenir version of the patch differs in only two major ways from the official. As always, it is smaller than the official emblem, measuring 3" in diameter. And, as is also quite common, the patch is not fully embroidered, but has a navy twill background in the center of the design. Better attention has been paid to detail in this patch than in many of the souvenir versions. Even the number of stars in the background is correct, along with the appropriate shades of blue in the body of the patch.

STS-41G was launched from the Kennedy Space Center on October 5, 1984, making it the thirteenth mission in the Shuttle series. It was the sixth flight of the Orbiter *Challenger*, and carried the largest crew of astronauts, flying in one spacecraft, up to that time. The seven crew members rocketed into orbit with a full slate of payload and experimental activities on their agenda. The crew included Robert Crippen, Commander; John A. McBride, Pilot; Kathryn D. Sullivan, Mission Specialist 1; Sally Ride, Mission Specialist 2 (making her second flight into space); David Leestma, Mission Specialist 3; Paul Scully-Power, Payload Specialist; and Marc Garneau, Canadian Payload Specialist.

Mission 41-G included a number of impressive firsts for the American space program. These included the first flight of a Canadian national (Garneau) as a Payload Specialist. His participation in this flight was made in partial repayment for Canada's contribution to the Shuttle Program, namely, the Remote Manipulator System (known in Garneau's homeland as CANADARM). This mission was also the first space flight to carry two women as members of the crew, and marked the first EVA by an American woman astronaut.

Kathryn Sullivan missed being the first woman to walk in space by less than three months. She was just edged out by Soviet cosmonaut Svetlana Savitskaya, who took a walk outside the Soviet space station Salyut 7 in July of 1984. Savitskaya's

EVA lasted for 3 hours and 35 minutes, as she performed welding duties on the exterior of the space station. Sullivan's went for 3 hours and 29 minutes. Her EVA demonstrated the first U.S. fuel transfer in space.

STS-41G also carried the first astronaut to fly four Shuttle missions, Commander Robert Crippen. The most experienced Shuttle Commander would fly his craft through the first re-entry profile of any shuttle flight to cross the Eastern United States. During the flight the crew deployed Nasa's Earth Radiation Budget Satellite (ERBS) and the Office of Space and Terrestrial Applications (OSTA-3) pallet payload. Other payloads included eight Getaway Specials, an IMAX motion picture camera, the Aurora Photography Experiment, and the Canadian payload, CANEX, which had been provided by the Canadian National Research Council.

The official patch of STS-41G is a 4" diameter round emblem with an additional sew-on tab at the bottom. This is the first NASA mission patch to have such a tag. According to official NASA statements the sew-on tag has become necessary due to the size of the crew. The claim (justifiable, to be sure) is made that there are too many names to fit comfortably and aesthetically on the main body of the emblem. In addition, rumor has it that the astronauts prefer that the patches be reserved for their use alone. One may note that only the names of the Payload Specialists appear in the tag of 41-G. The astronauts' names are all embroidered on the main body of the patch.

The official emblem and tag of 41-G are bordered by an overlock border sewn in silver mylar. The background of the tag and the banner at the lower edge of the patch is embroidered in navy blue. The crew's names are sewn in white. In addition, the red and white Canadian flag is embroidered next to Garneau's surname.

The mission insignia focuses on the seven crew members and the American flag. The flag dominates the upper part of the patch. It is depicted in a slightly furled position, as if it were waving from a mounted position. In the center foreground is the unity symbol known as the astronaut pin.

This pin is worn by all members of the astronaut corps. The pin design depicts a trio of trajectories, launching from earth, and merging in infinite space. They are capped by a bright shining star and encircled by an elliptical wreath which denotes orbital flight. The entire pin is embroidered in gold mylar thread and outlined in deep brown. In the background seventeen stars can be seen in the heavens. STS-41G was originally designated as mission STS-17. These stars are symbolic of that original designation. The artwork for this patch was done by Patrick Rawlings.

The souvenir version of the patch takes several liberties with the design for the sake of economy. First, the emblem is made as one piece. The sew-on tab of the official emblem is replaced in this version by a solid, shield-shaped cloth. The blue fields containing the astronauts' names are royal-blue twill. The overall size of this emblem is 3", which is also typical of the souvenir versions of the Shuttle patches.

The fourteenth flight in the Shuttle series was mission STS-51A. This flight left the Cape on November 8, 1984, carrying the Canadian satellite Anik D2 and the Hughes LEASAT 1 (SYNCOM IV-1). Both were communication satellites destined for geosynchronous orbits. This mission is especially notable for having retrieved the ill-fated PALAPA B-2 and WESTAR VI, which had been deployed by STS 41-B.

Failure of their upper PAM stages left them in useless orbits. The satellites are now back on earth. After their eventual repair, it is possible that they can be relaunched by the Shuttle. This represents another major advance that the Shuttle provides, since it could have the long-term effect of prolonging satellite life, thereby dramatically lowering the cost (and risk) of commercial satellite ventures.

STS-51A also carried a commercial experiment belonging to the 3M company. The Diffusive Mixings of Organic Solutions (DMOS) experiment was carried in the Orbiter's mid-deck. This was the first attempt to grow organic crystals in the microgravity environment of the Orbiter. 3M scientists are studying the crystals produced in this experiment for their optical properties and other characteristics that might have important applications to 3M's businesses in the areas of electronics, imaging and health care. At the Twenty-Second Space Congress held in April of 1985 in Cocoa Beach, Florida, Dr. Chris Podsiadly of 3M reported on the relative success of the experiment performed on 51-A. He noted that 3M is participating in microgravity experiments to see if "preparing items for space production makes the resulting product on the ground better." He further stated that 3M's goal is "to do good science, develop the product, and enter the profit mode as soon as possible."

3M Company has funded their own Space Research and Applied Laboratories in St. Paul, Minnesota (which is headed by Dr. Podsiadly), to pursue their interest in space experiments. Their success on mission 51-A prompted them to approach NASA about a ten-year agreement to provide berthing and equipment for future space missions. Thus, STS-51A once again underscores the new view of outer space which is presented by the Space Shuttle. That is, space is now something more than a frontier to explore—it is an asset we can exploit for the benefit of all.

Frederick Hauck was Commander of STS-51A. His Pilot was David Walker. Joseph Allen served as Mission Specialist 1; Anna Fisher was Mission Specialist 2; and Dale Gardner was Mission Specialist 3. This flight carried no Payload Specialists. Ms. Fisher earned the distinction of being the third American woman and the first mother to fly in space. Her husband, also an astronaut, would fly on mission 51-I, making them the first husband and wife to fly into space (although not at the same time).

STS-51A's official patch is an oval-shaped, 4" emblem. It is fully embroidered, and has a yellow-gold overlock border. A blue band at the outer edge of the patch contains the crew's surnames embroidered in white. The Mission Specialists' are sewn at the top, while the Commander's and Pilot's surnames are embroidered separately, at the bottom. This band is outlined on the inner side by a narrow band of yellow gold which matches the emblem border.

The inner spacescape depicts the Orbiter *Discovery* en route to earth orbit. It trails a patriotic band of red and white, and is superimposed over a soaring eagle, symbol of the United States. Like the eagle, *Discovery* soars as it heads into space. The trailing stripes, the blue band at the edge of the patch, and the presence of the eagle are designed to generate memories of America's history and traditions. Behind the majestic bird, the earth's horizon can be seen, shaded in light blue and swirls of white clouds. Two satellites orbit the globe amid a celestial scene. They are symbolic, at one time, of two events: the deployment of the two satellites in *Discovery*'s cargo bay; and the successful retrieval of the two crippled satellites recovered on the mission. The depiction serves as a further symbol of the versatility and value of the Space Shuttle system. The artwork for the official patch was done by artist Stephen R. Hustvedt.

The souvenir version of STS-51A is a good color duplicate of the official emblem. Like most souvenir patches it is smaller than the official emblem, and it is not fully embroidered. It has a royal-blue twill background, which is oversewn with the crew names and the center design. It is also slightly less detailed in the area of the eagle's beak and eye, as well as in the body of the Orbiter.

STS-51C was the fifteenth flight in the Shuttle series, and launched from the Space Center on January 24, 1985. This was the United States's first classified military manned space flight. The crew included Ken Mattingly, Commander; Loren J. Shriver, Pilot; Ellison L. Onizuka, Mission Specialist 1; James F. Buchli, Mission Specialist 2; and Gary E. Payton, Payload Specialist.

Officially, little was said or revealed about STS-51C, due to its classified nature. However, it is generally known that *Discovery*'s payload was an electronic monitoring (ie, spy) satellite that was deployed from the cargo bay and carried to its proper orbit by an IUS upper Stage. Gary Payton was the Air Force's first Manned Space Flight Engineer on this flight, and had prime responsibility for the military payload. This mission marked the first time that communications between Ground Control and the Orbiter were blacked out. The only news dispensed during the flight were occasional status reports indicating the general health and status of the crew.

The official patch of STS-51C returns to the format of the sew-on tag. Again, it should be noted that the only name on the tag is that of the Payload Specialist. The surnames of the Commander and Pilot are embroidered in red at the top of the main emblem. The Mission Specialists' surnames are sewn similarly at the bottom. The Flight Engineer's surname is applied to the tag.

The 51-C patch is the most military-looking of all Shuttle series patches. Its basic color scheme is black and gold. The center of the patch is dominated by a gold eagle with outspread wings. His wingtips extend just beyond the edge of the patch.

As a result, the official emblem has an oversewn type border rather than an overlock type. In the center foreground of the patch, an American shield is outlined in gold and sewn in red, white and blue. The Orbiter is depicted in silhouette on this shield, trailing a contrail of red, white and blue. Grasped in the eagle's claws are three arrows, symbolic of the military aspect of the flight.

The eagle symbol rests against a background made of a spoked wreath. There are seventeen spokes in the lower portion, reaching to the outer edge of the wreath. In the upper portion, five spokes reach outward to five gold stars embroidered in the wreath's edge. These stars are symbolic of the five crew members.

A smaller souvenir version of this patch duplicates the color of the official emblem quite well. Unlike the astronauts' version, this patch has an overlock border. And, as with other tab patches in the series, this emblem is made in one piece. The border effect at the bottom of the main emblem is created by embroidering a gold line across the bottom arc of the design. In addition, the background for this emblem is a black twill.

A larger souvenir version of STS-51C is almost exactly the same size as the official emblem. It is easily recognized, however, by its one-piece construction. Like its smaller counterpart, this emblem was cut from a solid piece of cloth. In addition, the patch has an overlock border surrounding the entire patch. Even the eagle's wingtips are kept inside the body of the patch by the border. Also, the gold threads in this souvenir emblem are of a much lighter shade than those of the official emblem.

Shuttle flight STS-51E was scheduled for a March 3, 1985, launch. The mission was to have flown the second TDRS satellite and Anik C-1, the ninth in a family of Canadian geosynchronous communications satellites, as well as two French mid-deck experiments. In fact, Patrick Baudry of France was scheduled to fly this mission as a Payload Specialist for France. Senator Jake Garn of Utah was also scheduled as a Payload Specialist on this flight, acting as an observer and performing experiments relating to space sickness. The mission had to be cancelled due to problems with the TDRS payload. NASA then decided to remanifest and reschedule mission 51-D to include some elements of the cancelled 51-E.

These cancellations and reschedules occurred so late in the launch cycle that the patches for mission STS-51E had already been produced. So, although the mission did not fly, there is an official (that is, made by NASA's contracted manufacturer for the official emblems) patch available. It carries the surnames of the scheduled 51-E crew, including the two Payload Specialists (Baudry and Garn) on a sew-on tab at the bottom. It also carries the name of the Orbiter originally scheduled for the flight, *Challenger*. The basic design of the patch was used a short time later on the remanifested 51-D mission. Its symbolism will be discussed in relation to that mission. One can note that a souvenir version of the never-flown 51-E was also made. As usual, it is smaller than the official version, and is not fully embroidered.

STS-51D was the fourth flight of the Orbiter *Discovery*. The mission lifted off from Kennedy Space Center on April 12, 1985, carrying Anik C-1 and LEASAT 3 satellites. This flight was originally scheduled for a March launch to deploy the LEASAT and retrieve the LDEF from Earth orbit. When STS-51E was cancelled, 51-D was remanifested and plans to retrieve LDEF were dropped (this is now scheduled for flight 61-I, planned for a September 1986 launch). In addition to the two satellites, STS-51D payloads included the Continuous Flow Electrophoresis System (CFES), the American Echocardiograph Experiment, two mid-deck student experiments and two Getaway Special canisters.

The CFES, a continuing commercial venture of McDonnell Douglas and Johnson & Johnson, enabled the second flight of a commercial passenger. Charles Walker made his second flight as a Payload Specialist, operating the electrophoresis equipment. One other very special cargo consisted of an assortment of simple toys intended to demonstrate the unique properties of space flight for elementary and junior high school students. These included a spinning top, three gyroscopes, a spring-wound flipping mouse, a paddle-ball, ball and jacks, a Slinky, a yo-yo, a Wheelo, magnetic marbles, and a spring-wound, friction-wheel car.

The 51-D crew consisted of Karol Bobko, Commander; Donald Williams, Pilot; Rhea Seddon, Jeffrey Hoffman, David Griggs, Mission Specialists; and Charles Walker and Jake Garn, Payload Specialists. Senator Garn became the first politician in space with this flight. He carried out numerous medical physiological tests and measurements during the flight. These were designed to detect and record changes the body undergoes in weightlessness. Scientists are hopeful that the results of the Senator's tests will help cure spacesickness on future missions. While not serious or fatal, it is as annoying as seasickness, and leaves one just as miserable. Attempts to cure or prevent it have strong support from the astronaut corps.

The STS-51D emblem is a remake of the original 51E emblem (which never flew). The patch is oval in shape and has an oversewn border. At the bottom, a sew-on tag is attached containing the names of the two Payload Specialists. The official version is fully embroidered.

The dominant design on the patch is an orbit formed by a colonial American flag which trails behind the Space Shuttle. The flag in orbit signifies the American presence in space and this country's preeminence in manned spaceflight as exemplified by the Shuttle. The Orbiter flies out of the U.S. flag to indicate that it comes from this country and the American people. The original thirteen-star flag serves as a symbol of continuity in technical achievement in this country since colonial times.

The Orbiter for flight 51-D was *Discovery*, named after two famous sailing ships from the historic past: Henry Hudson's *Discovery* attempted to search for a northwest passage between the Atlantic and Pacific oceans. Instead, he discovered Hudson Bay. The Orbiter's second namesake was Captain Cook's *Discovery*. Under her sails he found the Hawaiian Islands and explored southern Alaska and western Canada. *Discovery* is embroidered at the left edge of the colonial flag and flanked by two stars, symbols of her earlier incarnations.

The souvenir version of STS-51D is typical of patches of this type. It is not fully embroidered, but has a navy blue twill background. It is also smaller than the official emblem. The detail work on the Orbiter and the earth is not as extensive. And, as with other tabbed Shuttle emblem designs, this version is cut from one piece of cloth. The Payload Specialists' names are embroidered into the extended tab at the bottom of the emblem.

STS-51B was the seventeenth flight of the Shuttle series, and the second flight of the NASA/ESA spacelab. For those who are fascinated by the complex world of flight designation and numerology, it should be noted that this mission was designated B and followed mission D making it the *fourth* flight of NASA's fiscal 1985. In addition, this mission was also designated Spacelab 3, even though it was only the *second* flight of the Spacelab unit. So much for logical numbering systems.

51-B launched from the Kennedy Space Center on April 29, 1985. Spacelab 3 featured fifteen experiments in materials-processing, fluids mechanics, life sciences, atmospheric physics and astronomy. The seven-man crew was accompanied by twenty-four rats and two monkeys. The only problems incurred during the flight were minor (including a bout of spacesickness suffered by one of the monkeys) and all but one of the experiments yielded excellent results.

Despite NASA's announcement at the end of STS-9 (Spacelab 1) that no missions would operate continually, Spacelab 3 followed just such a program. Later Spacelab missions (Spacelab 2 on mission STS-51F and Spacelab D1 on STS-61A) would also operate on a continuous basis during the mission.

The crew of STS-51B included Robert Overmyer, Commander; Frederick Gregory, Pilot; Don Lind, Mission Specialist 1; Norman Thagad, Mission Specialist 2; William Thornton, Mission Specialist 3; Lodewijk van den Berg, Payload Specialist (materials science expert); and Taylor Wang, Payload Specialist (fluids expert). Their flight aboard the Orbiter *Challenger* lasted just over seven days.

The official emblem of STS-51B is a fully embroidered, 4″ diameter round emblem. At the bottom it has a sew-on tag containing the names of the two payload specialists. The entire patch is circled by a navy, overlock, ravel-proof border. A narrow inner band of pale yellow outlines a wider region of light blue. This area is bordered on the interior by a slim band of white. The astronauts' names are embroidered in this band of light blue. At the top of the emblem, the Spacelab 3 designation is sewn in red.

The Orbiter and its science module payload are featured in the center design of the insignia. The Shuttle is depicted flying through the Constellation Pegasus. Its seven stars surround the spaceship as it orbits a flag-draped earth. A deep-blue outline completes the shape of the constellation, allowing the viewer to see the winged horse streaking across the sky. The seven stars of Pegasus also serve as symbols of each of the seven crew members on this flight.

The artistic detail and color make this patch one of the prettiest in the Shuttle series. It was designed by Carol Ann Lind, wife of Mission Specialist Don Lind. The combination of colors in this emblem give it a very soft and beautiful appearance. From an aesthetic standpoint, it is one of the most collectible patches in the entire U.S. space program. Note the exquisite detail in the rendering of the Orbiter. Even the souvenir version of this patch does a creditable job of showing detail in the Orbiter's cargo bay.

The center of the souvenir patch is a navy twill material. This is not as attractive as the fully embroidered official version. Also missing is the light yellow band surrounding the edge of the patch. This omission only detracts from the overall look of the emblem. For those who wish to understand the design differences between the official and souvenir versions of space patches, this is an excellent example. Like other tabbed patches in the Shuttle series, this souvenir version is constructed as a one-piece emblem. The bottom portion of the patch border is sewn as a blue line of the souvenir version.

The eighteenth flight in the Shuttle series carried a French scientist and a Saudi prince into space. STS-51G was launched on June 17, 1985 from the Cape with a crew of seven. These included Daniel Brandenstein, Commander; John Creighton, Pilot; Shannon Lucid, Mission Specialist; John Fabian, Mission Specialist; Steven Nagel, Mission Specialist; Patrick Baudry (France), Payload Specialist; and Sultan bin Salman Al-Saud (Saudi Arabia), also a Payload Specialist.

STS-51G carried the largest satellite cargo to date into orbit. On board were the Morelos-A communications satellite (the first general communications satellite to serve Mexico), the Arabsat-A communications satellite (which belongs to the 22-nation Araba Satellite Communications Organization), the Telstar 3-D communications satellite (owned by AT & T), and the *Spartan* astronomy platform. The *Spartan* was deployed and retrieved after two days of free-flying observation. This was the first flight with two foreign nationals in the crew. It was also the third consecutive flight to have seven crew members.

The French crew member, Baudry, used the French Echocardiograph Experiment (FEE) to investigate the human cardiovascular system's adaptation to space. In addition, he conducted the French Postural Experiment. They measured electromygraphic activity of muscles, and head/eye movements in an effort to understand the effects of weightlessness on posture control. Al-Saud conducted 70mm photography of Saudia Arabia, including oil slicks, pollution, and fish communities in the Persian Gulf and Red Sea. He also conducted a fluids experiment investigating the separation of fluids, which included a sample of Saudi crude oil.

The 51-G patch is very well designed and particularly striking. It is a round, 4" diameter emblem. Like several of the most recent Shuttle patches, the surnames of the Payload Specialists are attached to the emblem with a separate sew-on tag. Also embroidered on this tag are the two flags of the foreign crew members. The French flag is sewn next to Baudry and the Saudi Arabian flag next to Al-Saud. In the main body of the patch, a red band encircles the main scene and contains the names of the other five crew members. All are embroidered in white. The patch is bordered by a gold, overlock, ravel-proof border.

In the center scene a golden eagle dominates the foreground, flying steadfast and determined into the future. Beyond, the Shuttle flies in formation on top of the Wright Flyer, which was the first vehicle to free man from the bonds of earth's gravity. The Flyer is reminiscent of America's first days of flight. The Shuttle serves as the symbol of our ability today, to strive for other worlds and new beginnings. The Orbiter rides above the antique plane, to show that each advance in the world of technology is carried by the accomplishments that have preceded it. Together, with the eagle, they look into the future towards America's continuing role as the world's leader in space exploration.

The background of the center spacescape is embroidered in a dark navy blue. The Wright Flyer and the Shuttle are both sewn in white. Grey, light blue, and black add shadow and detail. Each vehicle trails a light-blue contrail into the vast distance behind. Like the eagle, whose wings stretch for their upwards sweep, they are poised to soar.

The 3" souvenir version of the patch is sewn as a one-piece emblem on a field of red twill. The red background is several shades darker than the brilliant crimson of the official version. In addition, the contrail of the vehicles in flight is a grey to match the color of the vehicles. A second souvenir version is made in a larger 4" size. Like its smaller counterpart, it is cut from one piece of cloth, in a shield shape. While it is fully embroidered, it is not as true to the official emblem colors as the 3" version. The outer band is sewn in a rust-colored red in this version. In addition, the contrails of the Shuttle and the Wright Flyer are grey as they are in the 3" size. They are composed of numerous lines of embroidery instead of the solid bands which trail from the vehicles in the official version.

The nineteenth mission in the Shuttle series is STS-51F, which is also known as Spacelab 2. 51F launched from the Kennedy Space Center on July 29, 1985, and flew a seven-day mission. For the fourth consecutive mission, the Orbiter carried a seven-man crew which included: Gordon Fullerton, Commander; Roy Bridges Jr., Pilot; Karl Henize, Mission Specialist 1; Story Musgrave, Mission Specialist 2; Anthony England, Mission Specialist 3; Loren Acton, Payload Specialist 1; and John-David Bartoe, Payload Specialist 2.

This was the first pallet-only Spacelab flight. As a result, primary mission objectives were to verify the Spacelab systems and determine the interface capability of Spacelab and the Orbiter. A secondary objective of the mission was to obtain scientific and technology data that demonstrated Spacelab's capability to conduct investigations in a number of disciplines on a single mission. Thirteen investigations in seven scientific disciplines were chosen to exercise Spacelab's capabilities to the fullest and, at the same time, collect valuable research data. Once again, the duties of Spacelab required around-the-clock activity by members of the crew.

On a less serious note, this mission also carried the "Cola Wars" fight between Coca-Cola and Pepsi into space. Each company provided the crew with one or more containers of their respective beverages in containers especially designed for weightlessness. These "space cans" allowed the astronauts to drink carbonated soft drinks while in orbit, something they had been unable to do previously. The crew tasted Coke first, then Pepsi. This "Star Wars" version of the "Cola Wars" did not produce a victor. The astronauts expressed no preference for either brand. In fact, since the sodas could not be served chilled (no refrigerator in the Shuttle kitchen), the crew's reaction was best described as discreet and noncommittal.

The official patch of STS-51F is a fully embroidered, 4" diameter emblem. At the bottom, a sew-on tag contains the surnames of the two Payload Specialists, Acton and Bartoe. At the top, sewn in gold, is the mission designation, Spacelab 2. The astronauts' names are embroidered in white around the outer edge of the emblem.

The patch depicts the *Challenger* orbiting the blue-white marble of earth. The Orbiter is seen in a rear view with the bay doors in a closed position. Ahead, the sun shines brightly on the approaching spacecraft. Nineteen white stars are dispersed throughout the heavens, symbolic of the Shuttle flight number (this was, of course, the nineteenth flight in the series).

The background of the patch is fully embroidered in black, a symbol of deep space. The Orbiter is sewn in grey and silver, with black thread adding detail. These color choices produce an overall effect that is very subdued, which also seemed to be the tone of the entire mission. Even though it was a Spacelab flight, much less media attention was paid to this mission than others in the Spacelab series.

The souvenir version of 51-F is a 3" emblem. Like others of its kind, it is a one-piece emblem, incorporating the bottom tab into the body of the patch. The black background is twill in this version, but the overall color scheme is faithful to that of the official version. A larger souvenir version of this patch also foregoes the sew-on tab and is produced in a one-piece design. In this version, the Orbiter is sewn in a very bright white thread, as are the crew's names, the stars, and cloud detail over the earth. As a result, this version seems more lively, almost jumping out of the emblem. At the top, the Spacelab 2 designation and the sun are sewn in a burnt-orange thread, differing from the deep yellow gold of the official version.

The flight of STS-51I marked the twentieth flight in the Shuttle series as *Discovery* carried her crew skyward on August 27, 1985. Commander for the flight was Shuttle veteran Joe Engle. His Pilot was Richard Covey. Mission Specialist 1 was James van Hoften; Mission Specialist 2 was John Lounge; and Mission Specialist 3 was William (Bill) Fisher, spouse of STS-51A astronaut Anna Fisher. Fisher's flight made this pair the first married couple in space even though they were on separate flights.

Objectives for this mission included the repair and salvage of the lifeless Leasat/Syncom IV-F3 satellite on orbit and its redeployment for normal operation. The Shuttle also deployed the ASC-1/PAM-D for American Satellite Co., the AUSSAT-1/PAM-D for the Australian government, and the LEASAT IV-F4 satellite for the U.S. Navy. In addition, 3M Corporation's Physical Vapor Transport of Organic Solids (PVTOS) experiment flew in *Discovery*'s mid-deck. This was the third flight, in an ongoing series, for experiments of 3M. Crystals produced by PVTOS are being studied by 3M scientists to learn about their optical properties and other characteristics that might ultimately have important application to 3M's businesses in the areas of electronics, imaging and health care.

The official emblem for STS-51I is a 4" diameter round patch. No Payload Specialists flew this mission, and thus, no sew-on tab was incorporated into this patch design. Like all official emblems of the Shuttle Program, it is fully embroidered. The border is made of silver mylar and is an overlock, ravel-proof type. The astronaut's surnames are embroidered in white around the upper edge of the patch.

The crew patch for this mission is based on a strong patriotic theme. The basic colors are red, white and blue, suggesting the American flag. In addition, a dominant American bald eagle is depicted in aggressive flight. His body and wings are sewn in several shades of tan and brown. Details are outlined in gold mylar. The shock wave, the white line that surrounds the eagle, is symbolic of the one formed by the Orbiter during the entry phase of the flight. The white stars help create the impression of the flag, but they are also intended to suggest the mission designation. Unfortunately, there are only nineteen stars in the field above the eagle, and this was mission number twenty. This flight was to have been number nineteen, which is the reason for the error. By the time the patch was in production, the omission was overlooked and the second "nineteen designation" patch had been produced. As with Apollo 11, it was decided to ignore the error. Thus, all official 51-I patches are short one star.

The souvenir version of STS-51I is a 3" emblem. It, too, has a silver mylar border, but the background is created by navy twill, not embroidery. The color scheme follows that of the official emblem quite well. Because of its smaller size, and because it is not fully embroidered, the nineteen white stars nearly become thin lines of thread instead of the richly sewn symbols of the official version. It is quite pretty, however, and deserves a place in anyone's collection of space emblems.

STS-51J lifted off from the Kennedy Space Center on October 3, 1985. Like mission STS-51C before it, this mission was exclusively devoted to Department of Defense objectives. Launch and landing times, as well as flight duration time, were not announced in advance. This was the first flight of the final Shuttle in NASA's fleet, the *Atlantis*. This new Orbiter established a Shuttle high-altitude record by reaching a height of 320 miles shortly after lift-off.

The payload of STS-51J was classified secret by the U.S. Air Force, but it is generally considered that it consisted of two General Electric Defense Satellite Communications System (DSCS-3) spacecraft which were mounted on board a single IUS booster. The flight was commanded by Karol Bobko and piloted by Ronald Grabe. Robert Stewart and David Hilmers acted as Mission Specialists. The Defense Payload Specialist was William Pailes.

Just as preceding Shuttle missions have separated the Payload Specialists' names onto a sew-on tag, so does the STS-51J emblem. The official patch is a 4" diameter emblem which has the tag located at the bottom. The overall background of the emblem is light grey. The patch has a grey, overlock border, as does the additional tag. The astronauts' names are embroidered in dark grey around the edges of the emblem.

At the lower portion of the patch, the grey outer band rises up to form a representation of Liberty, symbol of our nation. She holds her blazing torch aloft as a symbol of the Shuttle's dual role in the realms of science and our nation's defense. Above her, the *Atlantis* orbits the globe, trailing a flame lit by Liberty's torch. Thus, she also serves as a reminder that the United States carries the light of freedom for the world. The flame of Liberty's torch and the Shuttle's engines are sewn in several shades of orange thread. The Orbiter is depicted in white with black detail against a background of solid navy blue. Below, the earth is seen in various hues of blue with white clouds. Liberty is a solid light grey. Detail is added with dark grey.

The souvenir version of STS-51J is a 3" emblem. It is cut and sewn from one piece of cloth, adding the Payload Specialist's name to the main body of the patch. The embroidered colors of the patch follow these of the official version quite closely. The background of the center scene is made of navy twill. There is no special symbol to signify that this is the twenty-first flight in the Shuttle Program.

STS-61A was the first flight of NASA's fiscal 1986. It was launched from the Kennedy Space Center on October 30, 1985. 61-A carried the fourth Spacelab flight, Spacelab D-1, the first German Spacelab. The "Deutschland" mission marks the first in a series of dedicated West German missions on the Space Shuttle. The D-1 is dedicated to experimental scientific and technological research which will be used by German and other European universities, research institutes and industrial enterprises.

Challenger carried an eight-member crew into orbit, making this the largest group to have ever flown in space. Commander for the flight was Henry Hartsfield (he was Pilot for STS-4 and Commander for STS-41D). Pilot was Steven Nagel, who served as a Mission Specialist on STS-51G. The crew also included Bonnie Dunbar, serving as Mission Specialist 1; James Buchli, Mission Specialist 2; Guion Bluford, Mission Specialist 3. Payload Specialists included Ernst Messerschmid and Reinhard Furrer of West Germany and Wubbo Ockels of the Netherlands. The mission was scheduled to fly for seven days. STS-61A is also the first Shuttle flight to require control of the payload from a location outside the United States.

The official emblem of STS-61A is well-designed and quite beautiful. It is a fully embroidered, 4" diameter round emblem. A sew-on tag is attached at the bottom which include the surnames of the three Payload Specialists. The outer edge of the patch and the background of the tag are formed by a field of white embroidery. Crew members' names are sewn into this background in navy thread. In addition, the patch is bordered in a navy, overlock border. The sew-on tag also includes a small ESA symbol, represented as a blue globe with a small e superimposed upon it. This insignia was worn by the eight crew members on their spacesuits.

In the center of the emblem, *Challenger* is depicted as she makes her second Spacelab flight. Inside the cargo bay she carries a long science module, which is sewn in red. From the right side of the Orbiter, a German flag creates a tricolor banner around the earth. It emerges from the far side as an American flag which completes the circle, joining its counterpart on the underside of the spacecraft. These two banners serve as a symbol of international cooperation and friendship. They circle the earth to symbolize the orbital nature of the flight, as well as the many and varied benefits space exploitation offers to all.

The souvenir version of STS-61A is not as striking as its official counterpart. This is primarily due to the fact that it has a background of white twill instead of the tight embroidery of the official patch. The colors of the souvenir version are a close match to those of the official emblem. It is smaller in size (3"), as is to be expected. And, like those before it, the sew-on tag is eliminated, making the emblem a one-piece construction which includes the names of the Payload Specialists.

STS-61B was launched on November 26, 1985. It was the second flight of the Orbiter *Atlantis*. The crew included Brewster Shaw, Jr., as Commander; Bryan O'Connor as Pilot; and Mary Cleave, Sherwood Spring, and Jerry Ross as Mission Specialists. Payload Specialists for the flight will be Charles Walker of McDonnell Douglas and Rudolpho Neri, the first spaceman from Mexico. He is flying as Payload Specialist for the Morelos-B satellite of the Mexican government.

The official emblem for STS-61B is a round, 4" diameter patch. It has a white, overlock border surrounding a band of deep, navy blue. At the bottom, a sew-on tag contains the names of the Payload Specialists. The Mexican flag is embroidered next to Neri's name. The crew's surnames are sewn in white around the upper edge of the patch. They are separated by gold stars.

The center spacescape depicts *Atlantis* circling a blue-white globe. At the edge of the world, a rainbow highlights an unfurled U.S. flag. The twenty-third flight in the Shuttle series orbits with her bay doors closed, on a heading towards her flag.

STS-61C was the twenty-fourth flight of the shuttle series. The Orbiter *Columbia* was launched after a refitting that took nearly two years. Launch date was December 18, 1985. The crew of *Columbia*'s first flight after its overhaul included Robert Gibson (Commander), Charles Bolden (Pilot), George Nelson (Mission Specialist), Steve Hawley (Mission Specialist), Franklin Chang-Diaz (Mission Specialist), Robert Cenker (Payload Specialist) and Congressman Bill Nelson (Spaceflight Participant).

Congressman Nelson is chairman of the House Subcommittee on Space Science and Applications. He became the second congressional observer to fly in the Shuttle (Senator Jake Garn of Utah became the first on STS-51D). Nelson represents the district, which includes Cape Canaveral and the Kennedy Space Center.

Congressman Nelson answered criticism, suggesting that he was making the ultimate "congressional junket," by making these comments before the flight: "I am thankful for this opportunity to fly because it is going to make me a better committee chairman. In the committee we have volumes of data thrown at us by witnesses, reports and so on, and we have to evaluate that as the committee that authorizes appropriations for the Space Program. I have learned so much in my weeks of preparation and training—things that I have never been exposed to before that give me a totally different frame of reference."

Other activities of mission 61C included Chang-Diaz's shuttle video. Chang-Diaz is a naturalized American citizen from San Jose, Costa Rica. During the flight, he made a videotape in Spanish which depicts life aboard the shuttle. The tape is to be distributed among Spanish-speaking groups in the United States and Latin America.

The main payload of STS-61C, however, was the Satcom Ku-1, a communications satellite owned by RCA Astro-Electronics. Robert Cenker is a senior staff engineer with that company, and, acting as an observer, he represented their interests. He also operated an infrared camera developed by RCA which obtained radiometric images of volcanoes, ocean currents, the moon and the cities of Honolulu, Hawaii; Houston and Galveston, Texas; Miami, Florida; and San Juan, Puerto Rico.

The official mission patch of STS-61C is one of the most beautiful of all the shuttle patches. It is a 4" emblem and is fully embroidered. A side view of the Orbiter dominates the center of the emblem. It is sewn in the familiar black and white, with grey added for shadow and aesthetic effect. The nose of the Orbiter forms the point of a series of multi-colored vectors as it "extends the envelope" of our knowledge of space. These vectors trail above and below the spacecraft in yellow, orange, and red. At their point, the largest is sewn in navy blue with gold borders.

STS-51C

The crew's surnames are sewn into this largest vector. The Commander's and Pilot's names are sewn in gold above the Orbiter. In the bottom portion, just below the spacecraft, are the surnames of the three Mission Specialists. An additional tab at the bottom of the emblem contains the names of the Payload Specialist (Cenker) and the Spaceflight Participant (Representative Bill Nelson). The lower portion of the patch emphasizes the American flag. At the top, golden stars glow against the deep blue of space, symbols of this great adventure. The entire patch is made with an oversewn border of light gold.

The 3" souvenir version of this emblem is as beautiful as its counterpart. Its colors are remarkably close to those of the official version apart from some minor shading differences in the background of the emblem. Both of these patches are prized by collectors for their exquisite beauty.

In July of 1985, Vice-President George Bush announced the end of a long search and competition. At that time, he named Ms. Sharon Christa McAuliffe as the first private citizen, the first teacher, to travel in space. Christa taught social studies at Concord High School in Concord, New Hampshire. She was chosen from over 10,000 applicants to join six other crew members on the twenty-fifth shuttle flight, mission STS-51L.

STS-51L was originally scheduled to fly in December of 1985. For various reasons, the launch date had to be pushed back to January of 1986. The initial January launch date was January 24, according to the NASA press kit for the mission. Delays caused by equipment difficulties and bad weather plagued the mission and the launch date was pushed back several times. Finally, on January 28, 1986, a bitter cold Florida morning, *Challenger* left her launch pad at Kennedy Space Center. Seventy-four seconds into the flight, at 11:39 A.M., something went horribly wrong. A malfunction, probably in one of the solid rocket boosters, ignited the external fuel tank, causing the Orbiter to explode. For the first time in the history of America's Space Program, we lost the crew of a spacecraft in flight. Seven crew members, Christa McAuliffe among them, were killed in an instant as a horrified nation watched on live television.

The names of the seven astronauts on *Challenger*'s fateful mission have already been immortalized. They include Francis R. "Dick" Scobee, Commander. He was a veteran of the shuttle program, having also flown on STS-41C.

Michael J. Smith, a Navy flier and veteran of the Vietnam conflict, was *Challenger*'s Pilot. This was to be his first shuttle flight.

Judith A. Resnik was serving as one of three Mission Specialists on this flight. She, too, was a veteran of shuttle flight, having previously flown on STS-41D.

Ronald E. McNair, the second black American in space, had previously flown on STS-41B. He was serving his second stint as a Mission Specialist on this flight.

Ellison S. Onizuka was a Lt. Colonel in the Air Force. He was born in Hawaii, and was the first Japanese-American to fly in space, having served as a Mission Specialist on STS-51C, just as he was on this flight.

Gregory B. Jarvis was a Hughes Aircraft engineer who had been selected as a Payload Specialist for this mission. He was to have worked with the TDRSS-B communications satellite, the main payload of this mission. This was his first spaceflight.

STS-61C

Christa McAuliffe's presence on STS-51L made it something special for all Americans. The first private citizen in space was someone with whom we all seemed to be able to identify. NASA had formed a special program, called Teacher in Space, to underscore the importance of her trip. There is a special patch to commemorate this event (see the chapter on shuttle-related patches). Christa was to perform experiments to demonstrate the effects of microgravity on hydroponics, magnetism, Newton's laws, effervescence, chromatography and the operation of simple machines. She was also to assist in operating three student experiments being carried aboard

Challenger. Indeed, it began to seem that STS-51L was the shuttle flight that belonged to the entire country's children and teachers.

Challenger's flight plan also called for Christa to teach live lessons from space to school children across America. Some selected schools would be able to communicate directly with the shuttle, thus having a "visiting teacher from space" come right into their classrooms. Thousands more would be prepared to watch on television sets in their classrooms as Christa taught their lessons from space.

There were two important payloads in *Challenger*'s cargo bay that morning in January. The first, TDRS-B, was to join TDRS-1 in geosynchronous orbit to provide high-capacity communications and data links between earth and the shuttle, as well as other spacecraft and launch vehicles. After deployment from the shuttle, an IUS powered by a solid rocket booster would have carried the satellite to its proper transfer orbit. TDRS-B (in conjunction with TDRS-1) would have provided real time coverage through the single ground station at White Sands, New Mexico for about 85% of each orbit of a user spacecraft.

The Spartan-Halley Experiment Package was designed as a free-flying payload, designed to observe Halley's comet during the 51L mission. Spartan-Halley was to be deployed from the *Challenger*'s cargo bay for 45 hours. It would have measured the ultraviolet spectrum of the comet using twin spectrographs designed and built by the Laboratory for Atmospheric and Space Physics (LASP) at the University of Colorado in Boulder, Colorado. The cameras and instruments of the experiment package were to analyze the active comet, looking for hydrogen and oxygen atoms; and carbon, nitrogen and sulfur molecules. Had any of these elements been detected, it would have been an indication of more complex compounds, which could be present in the ice and dust making up the comet's nucleus. The spacecraft would have been retrieved by the RMS of the *Challenger* and returned to earth in the cargo bay. Its loss ensures that the United States will have no spacecraft observations of Comet Halley.

The entire world mourns the loss of *Challenger* and her crew. Long after the explosion and destruction, Americans still feel the shock and horror they experienced that Tuesday morning. The destruction of the spacecraft and the loss of her crew have temporarily put further shuttle missions on hold. However, President Reagan, Congress, NASA and public opinion all support a continued manned space program.

Christa McAuliffe's back-up, Barbara R. Morgan of McCall-Donnelly Elementary School in McCall, Idaho has declared her determination to fulfill the dream of the first Teacher in Space: to bring the reality and importance of the space program to all of America's children.

Funds have been established for the children and spouses of the seven crewmembers. There is even a fund for the specific purpose of raising money to replace the lost *Challenger*. Replacement costs for the spacecraft are estimated to be approximately one and one-half billion dollars.

The tragedy of STS-51L has made it the most collected patch in the history of the space program. Each of us expresses sorrow and grief in our own way. Apparently the desire to touch, to feel, to experience this loss and crystallize it in the memory can best be fulfilled by touching a part of the experience itself. The mission patch has become a tangible symbol of that day's loss.

Like all official mission patches, it is fully embroidered and is 4" in diameter. It has an oversewn border of silver thread surrounding an inner field of white. At the top, sewn in black thread are the surnames of the three Mission Specialists: McNair, Onizuka and Resnik. At the bottom, sewn in the same shade, are the names of the Commander and Pilot: Scobee and Smith. The surname of the Payload Specialist, Jarvis; and the Spaceflight Participant, McAuliffe, are embroidered on a tab at the bottom of the patch. A red apple by Christa's name serves as a symbol of her profession.

The spacescape at the center of the emblem depicts the earth against the field of the American flag. The upper right area shows a silver mylar Comet Halley streaking through the heavens. It is, of course, a symbol of the Spartan-Halley study which was to be carried out on this mission. In the foreground *Challenger* trails a golden contrail from Kennedy Space Center into its orbital path. The bay doors are open in preparation for the TDRS-B deployment.

The 3″ souvenir patch of STS-51L is nearly as popular as the official version. It differs from the official in two major ways other than size. First, it is sewn with a background of white twill (not full embroidery). Secondly, the silver mylar of the comet is replaced with regular silver thread in the smaller version.

8 ▪ SPACE SHUTTLE PROGRAM "RELATED" PATCHES

There are a number of patches which relate to the Shuttle program or various missions, which cannot be classified as Program or Mission patches. For the most part, these are official patches, which relate to specific events or activities tied to the Shuttle program. They encompass a wide variety of projects and ideas. This chapter will examine and explain them in as much detail as is available.

The Shuttle Carriers of America patch was designed for the crew(s) of the 747 that ferries the Orbiters from Dryden to Kennedy Space Center. The patch is triangular in shape. It has a white twill background with a royal-blue overlock border. The center design depicts an Orbiter riding "piggyback" on a 747 ferry. Below the plane are the initials DFRC and JSC. These stand for Dryden Flight Research Center and Johnson Space Center. Johnson is the home base for the carrier crews.

The Shuttle Chase Team patch is a 4" diameter, round emblem. It is fully embroidered, with a red background encircled by a black, overlock border. Shuttle Chase Team is embroidered in white along the outer edges of the emblem. In the center, an Orbiter is depicted in its final landing approach upon return from orbit. Flying alongside is a T-38, one of NASA's chase planes. The chase planes ensure that the Orbiter's landing gear are extended, they check for tile damage, and generally "keep an eye on things" as the Shuttle makes its landing approach. This patch celebrates those unsung heroes who escort the "Space Truck" back to home base.

The Get Away Special patch is officially titled the Small Self-Contained Payloads emblem. It is a 4" patch with a grey twill background and a white, overlock border. The center is embroidered with a red, white and blue color scheme. The Shuttle is depicted trailing a band of red into the blue background of space. NASA and Get Away Special are embroidered in white. At the outer edge of the patch, the official name is sewn in royal blue.

The Get Away Special program is offered by NASA to anyone who wishes the opportunity to fly a small experiment aboard the Space Shuttle. The experiment must be of a scientific research and development nature. Get Away Specials are flown on a space-available basis. Requests for flight space must first be approved at NASA Headquarters in Washington, D.C. It is there that a proposed experiment is screened for propriety and scientific or technical aim. These requests must be accompanied or preceded by the payment of $500 "earnest money." When a request is approved it is assigned a payload identification number and referred to the Get Away Special Team at NASA's Goddard Space Flight Center located in Greenbelt, Maryland.

LDEF (the Long Duration Exposure Facility) was almost overlooked on Shuttle flight STS-41C.

The media coverage of the Solar Maximum repair pushed attention to LDEF onto the back burner. LDEF is a large structure, housing 57 scientific applications and technology experiments, currently in earth orbit. It was deployed on 41-C and will remain in orbit until late 1986 (STS-G1I is tentatively scheduled to retrieve it from orbit). LDEF experiments range in research interest from materials to medicine to astrophysics. All of them require free-flying exposure in space, but no extensive electrical power, data-handling or altitude control systems. Many of the experiments are relatively simple and some will be completely passive while in orbit.

The results of their exposure to the space environment will be analyzed when LDEF is returned to earth. The LDEF project is managed by the Langley Center for NASA's Office of Aeronautical and Space Technology in Washington, D.C. The LDEF patch is a black rectangle with a black overlock border. NASA is sewn in red at the lower left, LDEF in blue at the upper right. The upper left corner of the patch contains a blue, green and white globe, being circled by a Shuttle Orbiter and the LDEF itself. The cylindrical shape of LDEF is depicted with multicolored squares representing the many experiments on board.

OAST-1 flew on Shuttle mission STS-41D. The OAST-1 payload included advanced solar array technology that can be applied to the conversion of the sun's energy into electricity for use on future spacecraft. OAST-1 marked the first demonstration in space of a large, lightweight solar array that can be retracted and restowed once it has been deployed.

Responsibility for OAST-1 was shared by NASA Headquarters and three NASA Centers. Marshall Space Flight Center developed and managed the OAST-1 mission for the Shuttle Payloads Engineering Division of the Office of Space Science and Applications, NASA Headquarters. The development of the photogrammetric techniques used to acquire structural dynamics data was managed by the Langley Research Center in Hampton, Virginia. The Solar Cell Calibration Facility experiment was managed by the Jet Propulsion Laboratory in Pasadena, California.

The OAST-1 patch is a rectangular emblem with a black background and black overlock border. It is a fully embroidered emblem. At the top, in large colorful letters is the program name, OAST-1. At the bottom, a brief explanation is provided by the words NASA Solar Technology. The body of the patch depicts the Orbiter extending the Solar Array as it orbits the earth.

TDRSS is a series of three identical spacecraft, which will form a communications system. TDRSS-1 was launched on STS-6. TDRSS-B was lost in the explosion that destroyed the Orbiter *Challenger* on STS-51L. The TDRSS system will support the Shuttle and planned scientific and application mission requirements from a single ground station when it is fully in place. This will dramatically lower the costs incurred from upgrading and operating a worldwide tracking and communications network of ground stations. In addition to the Shuttle, TDRSS will be equipped to support up to 26-user satellites simultaneously.

It will also provide two basic types of service. The first is a multiple-access service which will be able to relay data from as many as 20 satellites simultaneously. In the second format, it will provide single-access service, which allows for two high data-rate communication relays. TDRSS does not process any data, in either direction. NASA describes it as "a bent-pipe repeater, relaying signals and data between the user spacecraft and ground terminal." The TDRSS ground station is located at White Sands, New Mexico.

The TDRSS patch is a large, triangular-shaped emblem. It has a background of white twill, trimmed with a royal-blue, overlock border. At the top, TDRSS is embroidered in blue. At the bottom, a red NASA is sewn over the phrase Communications for Space, which is embroidered in blue. Three circles in the center of the patch depict three aspects of TDRSS. The lower left circle shows the Shuttle deploying the satellite into earth orbit. In the lower right is a representation of the ground station at White Sands, New Mexico. Finally, in the upper circle, is the TDRSS itself, with its solar wings fully extended.

The MMU patch has its origins in Shuttle mission STS-41B. This mission served as the test flight of the Manned Maneuvering Unit (MMU) equipment. This patch is an illustration of that first test and subsequent applications.

This insignia was worn on the MMU itself during STS-41B. The astronaut is depicted in lone flight, at the controls of the unit. In the background, white stars are inset against the deep navy blue of outer space. A red vector cuts across the background of the emblem, symbolic of man's path to the stars. The MMU represents a new freedom for astronauts to work and live in space.

The MMU resembles its ancestor, which flew inside the Skylab Space Station in the 1970's. The MMU is a self-contained backpack powered by nitrogen gas propulsion. It allows astronauts to move outside the payload bay to other parts of the Orbiter or to other spacecraft. A good example is the retrieval of Solar Maximum on STS-41C. The MMU latches to the spacesuit (known officially as an Extra-vehicular Mobility Unit—or EMU) backpack and can be put on and taken off by an astronaut without assistance.

The Garn patch is Senator Jake Garn's personal patch, which he wore along with the mission patch on STS-51D. The patch has a rectangular bottom with a dome top. "Senator Jake Garn" is embroidered in white at the bottom, and acts as the foundation for a representation of the Capitol building in Washington, D.C. Above the building are symbols of the Senator's activities during the space flight.

These include a test tube, a strip of EKG paper, and a microscope, which were symbolic of the medical aspects of his flight. A gavel and an American flag serve as symbols of his legislative responsibility. The Orbiter is a symbol of the flight itself. Written in Latin around the upper edge of the patch are the words *Vigilantia Legum Latorum—Experimenta Medicinalia*. The English translation means Legislative Vigilance—Medical Experiments. This phrasing was supplied by the Library of Congress and suggests the Senator's twofold role in the flight.

First, he served as a legislative observer for the Senate. His task was to observe and report on the positive and negative aspects of the Shuttle program as he experienced it. Secondly, the Senator participated in medical experiments studying spacesickness during the flight.

The original artwork of the Senator's patch carried the designation STS-51E, the original flight Garn was to join. When that mission was combined with STS-51D, it had to be changed. Two patches were made with the flight designation STS-51D on them. Both flew with the Senator on the flight. The version that was mass-produced for distribution to NASA centers left off the mission designation.

A popular souvenir patch, relating to the Shuttle, is known as the Space to Grow emblem. It is a 3" patch depicting the Shuttle in earth orbit. A white twill band at the edge is embroidered with the message America Needs Space to Grow. The phrase, which is unquestionably one of a patriotic nature, suggests a subtle play on words. The obvious meaning is one of support for America's Space Program. The patch suggests that this country's future lies in the heavens. However, the play on words also looks back historically to the notion that growth is a necessity for the United States to remain a world leader. Unabashed supporters of the U.S. space efforts wear this patch with pride. NASA sources indicate that it has greatly increased in popularity since the tragedy of mission STS-51L. It seems to have become a symbol for those who favor a continuing U.S. Shuttle program.

The Mission Control Team Emblem was developed in recognition of this team's unique contribution to the Manned Space Program. These Manned Missions have succeeded because of the efforts of the Mission Control Team. The theme of the patch centers on the Sigma as the dominant symbol. This symbol was used once before, when it was painted on the side of a Mercury capsule (Mercury 8). It represents the total mission team. It also represents the individual flight-control teams from all programs past, present and to come. Within the Mission Control Teams, it is representative of all engineering, scientific and operations disciplines and tasks in support of the spacecraft and aircraft program elements. It can represent also many other things, such as the benefits to *all* mankind that are possible through space exploration and exploitation. The rocket launch represents the dynamic elements of space, which are the initial escape from our environment and the thrust of our curiosity to explore the universe. The energy of the program is, and must be, maintained by the mission team if the goals of the Space program are to be achieved.

The remaining elements of the patch are the earth, planets and stars. The earth, our home, will always be serviced by manned and unmanned spacecraft. Their object will be to improve the quality of life for everyone here on earth. The stars and planets represent a major source of scientific study. They are also symbols of the challenge of exploration for future Mission Control

Teams. The border of the patch is embroidered with symbols that represent the first three major programs to have been supported by the team: Mercury, Gemini and Apollo. The four stars represent later programs: Skylab, the Apollo-Soyuz Test project, the Earth Resources Aircraft Program and the Space Shuttle. When this patch was designed, all of these programs still lay in the future.

The wording of the patch stresses the attitude of the Mission Control Team to insure crew safety and mission success. Achievement Through Excellence is the translation from the Latin. It is the standard for those who work on the Mission Control Team. It represents the individual's commitment to a belief, to craftsmanship and perseverance. These qualities create a positive approach that assures mission success and the safe return of the crew. The patch thus recognizes the Mission Control Team's contribution to history.

The 25 MACH patch is worn only by a very select group of individuals. It is awarded to those astronauts who have flown in the Space Shuttle, for this is the only vehicle capable of 25 Mach (25 times faster than the speed of sound). The patch has a light-blue background and a blue oversewn border. A large 25 dominates the center of the patch. The Orbiter speeds by in the right foreground of the emblem, trailing a white contrail. Mach is embroidered in red inside the contrail.

This is an official patch which is (for obvious reasons) not available to the general public. Not even all astronauts qualify to wear this patch, since a ride in the Shuttle is a prerequisite to ownership.

9 ▪ INTERNATIONAL SPACE PATCHES

European Space Agency (ESA)

The only two world powers currently capable of independent space programs are the United States and the Soviet Union. In Europe, a number of nations have joined together to share technology, science, ideas and costs in order to have access to space, independent of the two superpowers. The rising cost of space exploration has forced every nation to "joint venture" their activities in space.

The Soviets and the Americans have also engaged in joint space missions with ESA countries and others around the globe. They have not flown another joint mission with each other to date, but the notion is being discussed extensively in scientific circles. ESA flies its own missions, with its own equipment, for member countries. It also has contributed to the development of Spacelab and Space Telescope, two major projects of the U.S. Space Program.

ESA's Spacelab Program patch is a 4" diameter round emblem. It has a white overlock border and a navy twill background. In the center, two astronauts are depicted at work in the Spacelab Module. The Shuttle orbits overhead, exhibiting the Module in its cargo bay. At the bottom, the program designation, Spacelab, is sewn in white. ESA and NASA are embroidered above, in the center design.

A second ESA Spacelab emblem depicts the flags of the European countries contributing to Spacelab. The center of the emblem is a small reproduction of the Spacelab Program patch. The flags are sewn in a circle around the outer background of the emblem. Twelve member-nations are represented on the patch. At the bottom, ESA and NASA are embroidered alongside the ESA logo.

The ESA Ariane patch is very similar to the Spacelab "flag" patch. It is very nearly a duplicate design. At the bottom, Ariane ESA is embroidered with the ESA logo. As with the previous emblem, the flags of participating Ariane users are displayed around the edge of the patch. Ariane is ESA's Expendable Launch Vehicle. The Ariane will place a satellite payload into orbit, but is flown only as an unmanned vehicle. The rocket is not reusable, like the Shuttle, hence the expendable designation. The Ariane rocket is depicted in the center of the emblem, lifting its payload beyond the distant horizon, into earth orbit.

Spacelab 1 is ESA's mission patch for Shuttle flight STS-9, which carried the first Spacelab into orbit. The patch has a maroon edge and border surrounding a navy-blue background. It is a fully embroidered emblem. Depicted in the foreground, the Shuttle orbits the earth with its bay doors open. Inside, the Spacelab 1 configuration can be seen. NASA and ESA are embroidered at the aft end of the Orbiter, identifying the cooperative nature of the mission. The mission designation is sewn along the horizon of the globe. A red vector signifies the launch and landing areas for the Shuttle, while a blue TDRSS leaves a contrail as it orbits the earth.

Spacelab 3 was the second Spacelab Mission. It flew on STS-51B. The patch has eight sides, but is rectangular in its overall shape. It has a blue background with a silver border. The earth is embroidered in blue and black at the left side of the design. Dominating the center, a very detailed Orbiter exhibits the Spacelab configuration from its open cargo bay. The mission designation, Spacelab 3, and the NASA logo are embroidered in white. Microgravity is sewn in gold just above the Orbiter, signifying the major experimental direction of this Spacelab mission.

Spacelab 2, the third Spacelab mission, flew on STS-51F. It is one of the most beautiful patches ever made. The emblem is triangular in shape and has a black overlock border. At the top, a black band is embroidered with white lettering for the mission designation. An inner triangle of blue contains the words Astronomy, Physics and Biology, the three major areas of research for this mission. The inner spacescape depicts an Orbiter in shadow and seen from above. The cargo bay is open, exhibiting the Spacelab cargo. In the upper left, the edge of the home planet can be seen. The sun dominates the patch, radiating brilliant hues of yellow, orange, red and magenta throughout the background of the design.

The ESA Space Telescope patch is symbolic of ESA's involvement in this U.S. project. ESA is contributing about 15% of the cost of this project in return for 15% observation time for European astronomers. ESA nations have contributed funds and hardware to this project. Space Telescope is designed to park in earth orbit and make celestial observations without the interference of earth's atmosphere. It will be able to observe many, many times the phenomena of the most powerful telescopes on earth. The center of the emblem depicts the Telescope with its solar array extended. The NASA logo is sewn above it, the ESA logo below. The Space Telescope Project designation forms an arc around the top of the inner design. The outer background of the emblem is a grey twill. Like other ESA patches it is embroidered with the flags of the project's member countries. The ESA logo is sewn at the bottom.

Olympus 1 is a large oval patch. It is embroidered on a blue twill background and has a blue overlock border. Olympus 1 is scheduled for launch by either Ariane or the Shuttle in 1986. It is the first in a series of satellites designed to provide extensive telecommunication abilities to the European nations. The satellite is sewn in brown and gold threads on the left side of the patch. The project name is sewn above it, while the ESA name and logo are embroidered at the lower right. Once again, flags of the ESA countries are embroidered on the upper and lower right edges of the patch.

Eureca is the acronym for the European Retrieval Carrier. ESA considers this project to be a Spacelab follow-on program and is scheduled for launch in the Shuttle some time in 1987. Eureca is a free-flying, retrievable platform. Like the U.S. LDEF, and the German SPAS, Eureca will carry experiments into earth orbit for later retrieval. Unlike its predecessors, Eureca will be supplied with electric power by solar arrays, which will make it more versatile. Eureca 1 will be devoted to materials and life-sciences research in microgravity. ESA is hopeful that Eureca will become self-supporting. The agency is considering a second Eureca which would be adapted for earth observation, electrophoresis and general science.

The Eureca patch is an oval emblem with a grey twill background and a grey overlock border. The project name is embroidered at the top, and the ESA logo at the bottom. At the edge of the emblem, again, are the flags of the project's member nations. The center of the patch depicts the satellite as it will look when deployed in orbit. The solar arrays are extended and experiment modules are exposed to space. Below in the distance, the Shuttle can be seen orbiting the earth, its task complete.

ESA's Earthnet emblem is a 4" diameter round patch. It has a light-blue twill background and a matching blue overlock border. In the upper left, the flags of the project member nations are sewn against the background. The project name and ESA logo are embroidered below them. Superimposed on the orbiting world below is the Earthnet "window" featuring closeup topography of the European continent. Mounted at the top of the windowed structure is an Earthnet antenna. This communication network will provide data-link and communication service throughout the European nations.

The Canadian Astronaut Program

There are currently eight patches (or "crests" as they are known in Canada) in the official Canadian Astronaut Program series. Since Canada has two official languages, English and French, each of the patches is labelled in both tongues.

Canada has a very extensive space program. Canadians have been involved in a number of ESA projects, and a Canadian firm (Spar Aerospace) built the Remote Manipulator System (RMS) called the CANADARM as Canada's contribution to the Space Shuttle. Canada has developed an astronaut program called the Canada Astronaut Program. Canada's first man in space was Marc Garneau, who flew on the STS-41G Shuttle mission and became an instant national hero. Canada has also committed itself to the space station. Its other astronauts are scheduled to flights beginning in 1986.

The Canadian Astronaut Program logo patch is a 4" diameter round emblem. It is fully embroidered with a white background and has a red overlock, ravel-proof border. The name of the program is sewn in English and French around the edge of the patch. The center of the patch contains a stylized maple leaf, the national symbol of Canada. A black dot in the center of the leaf makes it at the same time the symbol of a man. The stem of the leaf becomes his legs, while his arms are formed by the lower portion of the leaf design. The symbol thus represents both Canada and her astronauts.

A 3" diameter astronaut patch bears the familiar symbol of the stylized maple leaf against a white background. This patch has no lettering. The astronaut/maple leaf stands above an earth sewn in three shades of blue. The patch is bordered by a black overlock border. This emblem is a symbol of the Canadian astronaut and bears no explanatory language. The pride of the Canadian program is celebrated visually by the dominant symbol in the center of the emblem.

There are two official versions of a Space Shuttle Canadian Astronaut emblem. The first is a 4" diameter emblem. It is fully embroidered and has a silver overlock border. The background is embroidered in black to symbolize space. At the bottom portion of the patch, a blue and white earth turns beneath a Space Shuttle and a spacewalking Maple Leaf astronaut. The Orbiter's cargo bay is open, displaying its payload. Extended out and to the front of the Shuttle is Canada's contribution, the RMS. In the background, white stars can be seen shining in the distant heavens. At the edges of the patch, the English and French program designation is embroidered in white.

The 3" version of this emblem is an almost exact duplicate of the larger one. The black background is twill, not embroidered, but the design is the same. The lettering in this version is sewn in gold. The smaller size was designed to be worn on caps, hats, and sleeves. Slight color changes were made in order to distinguish it from the larger version.

There are two rectangular patches in the Canadian series, which mean exactly the same thing. Both have a fully embroidered white background, and both are bordered by a red, overlock, ravel-proof border. In both versions the first line of type is sewn in blue, while the second is sewn in red followed by a small black star (symbol of Canada's official space patches). The difference in these two patches is, of course, that one is produced in English and one in French. Both of them say Space Team on the first line, and Canada on the second. Naturally, they are called the Space Team Canada patches, and are differentiated only by their respective languages (the French version is slightly larger in size because the French words take more space to write).

The Canadarm patch is a hand-cut, uniquely shaped emblem. It is fully embroidered and has a white oversewn border. The background is bright yellow in color. This patch celebrates Canada's contribution to the Space Shuttle, the RMS or "Shuttle arm," as it is sometimes called. The patch depicts the Space Shuttle flying directly at the observer. Extending above the Orbiter and towards the viewer the "arm" dominates the upper portion of the patch. Canadarm is embroidered in red across this top portion. The d in the word is capped by a red maple leaf, symbol of the nation.

Last, but far from least in this country's space emblem series, is the Canadian Shuttle Mission Patch. This emblem celebrates the first flight of a Canadian astronaut. Marc Garneau made his first flight aboard the Shuttle *Challenger* on mission 41-G in 1984. He was the first foreign national to ride in America's Space Shuttle, though several have flown since. This patch is known in Canada simply as the Garneau patch.

Leonardo da Vinci's man was chosen as a symbol for Garneau's patch because of the variety of scientific disciplines examined by the Canadian experiments of STS-41G. Garneau conducted ten experiments covering three main categories: Space Technology, Space Science and Life Sciences. The overall color scheme of the emblem is blue and silver. Garneau's name is at the top, flanked by two Canadian flags. The designation Space Flight 1 is embroidered on both sides of the patch in Canada's two languages. A small star and copyright logo identify the patch as one of Canada's official space emblems.

It is important to note that all the designs related to the Canadian national program have been copyrighted by the National Research Council (NRC) of Canada, which is the Canadian equivalent of NASA. These designs may not be reproduced without permission. Only those sold with the official trademarks are authentic.

French Astronauts

The first French astronaut was Jean-Loup Chretien, who flew aboard a Soviet Soyuz mission in 1982. He conducted experiments, using a French Echocardiograph that was also used on STS-51G. Chretien rode in Soyuz T-6 with two Russian cosmonauts to a rendezvous with the Soviet space station, Salyut 7. During their stay in the station the T-6 crew performed many extensive and difficult medical experiments for French scientists back on earth. The Frenchman won the title of Hero of the Soviet Union, the Order of Lenin and a Gold Star from the Russian government.

Patrick Baudry was the backup for Chretien's 1982 flight. When the opportunity arose for a French astronaut to fly in the Space Shuttle, he was chosen as prime astronaut with Chretien serving as backup. Baudry was originally scheduled to fly as a mission specialist on the ill-fated 51-E mission. When it was finally cancelled and combined into the manifest for STS-51D he was bumped from the Bobko crew. The McDonnell-Douglas electrophoresis drug-purifying system was already installed in *Discovery*, and there was not enough additional locker space for Baudry's medical equipment. He was eventually rescheduled and flew on the STS-51G. Like Chretien, Baudry used the French Echocardiograph Experiment to investigate the human cardiovascular system's adaptation to a space environment. He also conducted the French Postural Experiment. This experiment measured electromygraphic activity of muscles and head/eye movements in an effort to understand the effects of weightlessness on posture control.

In addition to the STS-51G patch (and the cancelled 51-E's patch) Baudry wore a patch of French design as well. The patch is a fully embroidered emblem, 3½" in diameter. It has an overlock border of gold mylar. The center of the patch is dominated by the Shuttle *Discovery* flying against the background of space. It is flanked by an American and a French flag. The language of the patch is French. Sewn at the top is the phrase 1st French-American Mission. At the bottom is CNES the French Space Agency, and NASA, the American counterpart. Baudry's name is centered between the two. The lettering is sewn in white against a dark blue background. Four gold mylar stars separate the names.

10 ▪ THE FUTURE: THE YOUNG ASTRONAUTS PROGRAM™

NASA has long been a supporter of programs which encourage America's youngsters to study mathematics and science. The Space Agency's administration wisely recognizes the growing need for scientists, technicians, mathematicians and skilled professionals who have the ability to work in a space environment. Projects like the Space Station, renewed manned flights to the moon, a manned mission to Mars and other ideas as yet undreamed will require that thousands of today's young people understand the technologies of tomorrow.

NASA has allowed student experiments to be flown in the Shuttle, sponsored young people's attendance at Shuttle launches, funded educational programs, including the Teacher in Space program. High school teacher, Christa McAuliffe, was selected as the first "teacher in space." All of this activity has been focused on one basic notion: the development of future talent for this country's continued exploration and utilization of the space environment. NASA is not alone in efforts to encourage education in the sciences. Many American leaders in government education and industry recognize the need for qualified, educated individuals who can lead the United States into the twenty-first century.

The most extensive program aimed at promoting young people's interest in space endeavors is the Young Astronauts Program.™ * The concept of Young Astronauts™ was first conceived and developed by the syndicated columnist Jack Anderson. Mr. Anderson took his idea to the White House and presented it to President Reagan, who offered his enthusiastic support and consented to be Honorary Chairman. The Young Astronauts Program™ was officially launched on October 17, 1984 in the Rose Garden of the White House.

A private sector initiative, it is administered by the Young Astronaut Council. The Executive Committee of the Young Astronaut Council is composed of Jack Anderson, Chairman; Hugh Downs, Vice-Chairman; and Harold Burson, Secretary.

The Young Astronaut Council's plans include international cooperation between Young Astronauts Programs™ of many nations. Canada has become the first to set up its own Young Astronauts Program.™ It will be modelled on the U.S.'s program but have its own agenda and its own patches.

In the United States, the Young Astronauts Program™ helps to provide a national educational program aimed at elementary and junior high

TM & © 1985 YOUNG ASTRONAUT COUNCIL. All Rights Reserved. YOUNG ASTRONAUTS™ and YOUNG ASTRONAUTS PROGRAM™ logos and emblems are trademarks of the YOUNG ASTRONAUT COUNCIL.

school students. All children in grades 1–9 are eligible to become members if they pledge to give "my best effort to improve my grades in science, mathematics and related subjects, to learn about space and to help others towards these goals."

The program aims to equip students at an early age with the skills and knowledge necessary to adapt to the highly technological future "hurtling towards us whether we are ready or not" (the words of Jack Anderson on the first anniversary of the program). Science and mathematics are combined with learning about the U.S. Space Program to arouse students' curiosity and inject fun into the learning process.

A typical Young Astronauts™ chapter has about thirty student members. These chapters are usually set up in schools or community organizations such as churches, civic clubs and even local businesses. If a youngster lives in an area where no formal chapter yet exists, he or she can join as a "satellite" member until a formal chapter is formed.

The Young Astronauts Program™ is funded completely by the private sector. A number of major corporations are national sponsors and contributors. These include Pepsi-Cola USA, Commodore Computers, Marvel Productions, Martin Marietta Aerospace Corporation, Safeway Stores, Group W, Tymnet, Xerox Corporation, Coleco, Adidas and Rockwell International.

Several companies have been designated as official licenses of various Young Astronauts™ products. Action Packet Inc. of Ocala Florida is producing the Young Astronaut Program™ patches. Coleco is producing the Young Astronaut Cabbage Patch kid and Adidas will produce Young Astronauts™ activewear. Model and science kits will be produced by Monogram Models. All royalties go to help fund the Young Astronaut Program.™

The fundamental activity of the Young Astronaut Council is the development and distribution of educational material to chapters and satellite members. The materials developed by the Council are reviewed by a number of educational organizations and associations.

These include the American Federation of Teachers, the National Aeronautics and Space Administration (NASA), the Association of Science and Technology Centers, the National Air and Space Museum of the Smithsonian Institution, the National Council of Parents and Teachers, the National Science Foundation, the National Education Association, and many, many more.

In addition to an educational curriculum, Young Astronauts™ chapters also work with a wide selection of "activity packages." These include mathematics and science competitions, art and writing projects, model rocket kits and other science oriented products. Young Astronauts™ who win Program competitions are rewarded with such prizes as trips to Space Camp and Shuttle launches. Most chapters participate in Astronet, an electronic mail system which provides information on the U.S. Space Program as well as supplemental educational material and a monthly newsletter *Astrobits*.

Although the Young Astronauts Program™ is barely a year old, thousands of chapters have sprung up across the United States. In addition, the Young Astronauts Program™ is going international. The Young Astronauts™ of Canada is currently under development as are groups in Europe and around the world.

There are currently three patches which officially represent the Young Astronauts Program.™ The first of the three emblems is the original Young Astronauts Program™ patch. It is the first official trademarked design of the Young Astronaut Program.™ A second, irregular shaped, graphically very appealing logo has been trademarked and is expected to be used extensively on Young Astronauts™ apparel and products.

The first patch is round, approximately 3½" in diameter. It is a fully embroidered emblem and has a royal-blue overlock border. At the top of the patch the program name Young Astronauts Program™ is sewn in red against a white background. Along the lower edge, separated by three blue stars on each side, is sewn (in royal blue) United States of America. A thin blue line encircles a central spacescape which depicts symbols of Young Astronauts™ goals. A spacesuited astronaut performs an EVA above a grey lunar surface. The faceplate of the suit reflects only the depths of space. A Space Shuttle orbits above the right shoulder, while the Space Station is depicted above the left. The background is sewn in black to indicate deep space. The overall color scheme of the patch is red, white and blue, representing the United States.

The second logo depicts the Space Shuttle flying through several red, white and blue rings. Young is sewn inside a red ring just above the Shuttle's cockpit area. Astronauts appears in large blue letters just below it. It dominates the center of the emblem.

The third design is a modern graphics presentation of an A which is sewn in red and blue against a white twill background. The A is the program symbol for astronaut. Young is sewn in white letters at the bottom left leg of the A. Below it, a red stripe caps the word Astronauts which is sewn in blue. It is underlined by a second stripe, also sewn in blue.

All three of the Young Astronauts Program™ patches are registered trademarks. They may not be reproduced or copied without permission of the Young Astronaut Council or its authorized representative.

11 ▪ INDIVIDUAL PROGRAM AND EVENT PATCHES

NASA celebrated its twenty-fifth anniversary during the year 1983. The civilian space agency was born out of the older National Advisory Committee on Aeronautics (NACA). This patch was commissioned in honor of the event. It is a square emblem with a fully embroidered white background. The border is a white overlock style. NASA is embroidered in silver letters at the top, as is the date, 1958–1983, at the bottom. The color is symbolic of the anniversary number. In the center, a large 25 designates the anniversary number, as well. The white star along with the red and blue coloring of the 25 suggests our nation's flag and NASA's commitment to be a leader in space exploration. The patch has a simple design and few colors, but is very attractive, nonetheless. It is very popular with collectors and NASA personnel.

Pioneer 10, launched on March 3, 1972, was the first spacecraft placed on a trajectory to escape from the solar system into interstellar space. It was also the first to enter the Asteroid Belt and the first to fly beyond Mars and Jupiter. Its journey through the Asteroid Belt proved that this area of space contained far less material than previously believed. This meant that the Belt presented little hazard to manned or unmanned spacecraft. In its journey past Jupiter, Pioneer 10 provided us with the first photographs of Jupiter's Great Red Spot, as well as pictures of its moons: Ganymede, Callisto and Europa.

In February of 1976, it crossed the orbit of Saturn. In June of 1983, the spacecraft encountered the orbit of Neptune and became the first man-made object to leave our solar system. It should encounter a new solar system about once every million years.

Pioneer 10 was built by TRW and managed by NASA's Ames Research Center in California. In June of 1983, TRW commissioned a special patch commemorating the spacecraft's journey "beyond the planets." The patch is embroidered on black twill and has a yellow-gold overlock border. Pioneer 10 is embroidered in gold at the top. The message "first beyond the planets—June, 1983" is sewn in white around the outer edge. The interior of the patch depicts the Pioneer spacecraft as it passes Neptune, heading for the stars. The TRW and NASA logos are sewn in red alongside the craft.

This patch is not widely available, although most NASA Visitor Centers have it. It was originally made for use by TRW, but renewed interest in Pioneer 10 in 1983 led to its eventual disbursement throughout NASA channels.

Project Viking was a program that sent two unmanned vehicles to Mars. The Viking Landers reached the Martian surface in July and September of 1976. They sent back over 4,500 pictures of the Martian surface while their Orbiters returned well over 50,000. The Viking spacecraft carried instruments that allowed TV photography, high-resolution imaging, water detection, infrared thermal mapping, and the collection of data on the red planet's size, gravity, density and other physical characteristics. The prime contractor for construction of the Vikings was Martin Marietta Corporation. The project was managed by NASA's Langley Research Center in Hampton, Virginia.

The Viking patch is a 4" diameter round emblem. The border is oversewn in black on a mustard-yellow twill background. The center spacescape depicts a Viking Lander resting on the Martian surface. Above it, in Mars orbit, the Viking Orbiter relays signals from the Martian surface back to earth, which can be seen in the distance. A black background represents interstellar space. The patch is made in the biological symbol for man to underscore a main objective of the Viking mission: to determine whether there is microbial life on Mars. This question is still debated today, because results of Viking data in this area are still considered inconclusive.

The Voyager Project was conceived in the early 1960's as an unmanned mission to the outer planets (Jupiter, Saturn, Uranus, Neptune and Pluto). The two *Voyager* spacecraft were designed, built and operated by NASA's Jet Propulsion Laboratory in Pasadena, California. Launch was accomplished in the late summer of 1977. The two craft completed their fly-bys of Jupiter and Saturn in mid-1981. *Voyager 2* encountered Uranus in January of 1986. It will reach Neptune in August of 1989. Both spacecraft use telescope-equipped TV cameras and other instruments to study the outer planets, their moons, "rings" and atmospheres. *Voyager* discovered seven new moons orbiting Uranus as it "flew by." Congressman Bill Nelson has suggested they be named for the seven lost crew members of STS-51L.

The *Voyager* patch is a 4" oval emblem. Like most official NASA emblems it is fully embroidered. The patch is bordered with a red overlock, ravel-proof border. Depicted against a blue background, a *Voyager* craft is shown completing its Saturn fly-by. Trailing behind the spacecraft is a white contrail which spells *Voyager* and leads far back into space to the home planet earth. Jupiter is sewn between the earth and Saturn, as a symbol of *Voyager*'s first stop on its interplanetary journey. The craft's future stops at the edge of the solar system are not known. We are to assume that the spacecraft will continue beyond our sight to the planets beyond.

The Navstar Global Positioning System (GPS NAVSTAR) is an Air Force Project that is being built by Rockwell International Corporation. Navstar is an acronym for Navigation System Using Timing and Ranging. Each satellite in the Navstar system has a highly accurate atomic clock built into its hardware system. This clock enables the satellite to take very accurate measurements of an object's velocity (thus giving it potential applications in the area of weapons delivery). Navstar satellites are grouped in strategic orbits around the globe, and operate as teams. A radio receiver and computer system on earth can lock onto Navstar signals and get a "fix" on any point on (or near) the earth in either a horizontal or vertical plane. It is an extremely accurate system. It can be used by infantry, ships, aircraft, spacecraft and ballistic missiles.

The GPS NAVSTAR patch is a large triangular-shaped emblem. It is sewn on a blue twill background and has a blue overlock border. In the lower portion of the patch, the program's acronym is embroidered in blue. Below it, Global Positioning System is embroidered in black.

These phrases are set against the light-blue globe sewn into the background. The globe is marked with white lines of longitude, implying the navigational aspect of the GPS. At the top of the emblem, a large eight-pointed star serves as the symbol of the Navstar navigational system. Four Navstar satellites orbit in formation around it. Behind the star is a second globe, symbolic of the Navstar's ability to "blanket" the earth for navigational positioning data.

On January 28, 1986, NASA sent the first Space Flight Participant into orbit aboard the Space Shuttle. This is a new designation for Shuttle passengers, and is used to denote crew members who are not Command, Pilot, Mission Specialist or Payload Specialist. The SFP is, mainly, just an observer on Shuttle flights; and, not an active participant in activities of the other crew members. NASA's decision to fly a teacher as the first SFP on flight STS-51L had important consequences for the young people of the U.S. Christa McAuliffe, a thirty-seven-year-old social studies teacher from New Hampshire, taught at Concord High School. She was selected from among thousands of hopeful teachers across the

United States to be the first educator to fly in space.

A patch commemorating this event was designed by Bob Schulman, Chief of Community and Special Services Branch of NASA Graphics. It was already a popular collectible of students and teachers and has begun to involve more "non-space" people in learning about space. It has become even more popular as a collectible since the tragedy of January 28, 1986; and the loss of the *Challenger 7*. Christa McAuliffe's two lesson plans "The Ultimate Field Trip" and "Where We've Been, Where We're Going" will never be taught. But her backup for STS-51L, Barbara Morgan, has announced her determination to continue the Teacher in Space program.

The Teacher in Space patch is rectangular in shape and fully embroidered. A futuristic spacescape is centered against a white background. At the top the words Teacher in Space are embroidered in black. NASA is sewn in the same shade at the bottom. A light-blue overlock border wraps the edge of the emblem.

The inner space scene depicts the Space Shuttle in flight as it carries the first teacher into orbit. An orange contrail flows back to earth, a symbolic tie to the home planet. In the foreground, a flaming torch symbolizes the light of knowledge and education being carried by this first individual. Its message is encouragement to reach out and share the experience of education. Once shared, it can then be passed on to future generations. In the background, blue and white stars shine against the backdrop of interstellar space.

The Hubble Space Telescope is scheduled for launch in 1986. It is named after Edwin P. Hubble, noted astronomer and creator of the Big Bang theory of creation. NASA has described the Space Telescope as "the most important scientific instrument ever flown."

It will be carried into earth orbit by the Space Shuttle. Once in place, scientists on earth will be able to observe quasars, remnants of supernova, Seyfert galaxies, black holes and other phenomena of astronomy in more detail and completeness than ever before possible. Space Telescope will see objects 50 times fainter and 7 times farther away than anything visible from even the best earth-based telescopes. Astronomers will view the distant universe as it was 14 billion years ago, adding much to our knowledge.

It will be operated by the Space Telescope Science Institute located in Baltimore, Maryland. ESA has partly funded its construction, and European astronomers will have access to its incredible power. Lockheed Missile and Space Company is the main NASA contractor for the telescope and its support systems.

The Hubble Space Telescope patch is a fully embroidered rectangle. It is bordered with an overlock type, sewn in gold. The patch depicts the Space Telescope gazing at distant stars from its earthly orbit. In the lower left, the Shuttle circles the earth after completing the Telescope deployment. A spiral galaxy and the Milky Way are embroidered against the black background of space. The project name is sewn in gold at the top of the patch. NASA is embroidered in white at the lower right.

Galileo is a Jupiter Orbiter and probe that began as a follow-up project to the Voyager missions. It is hoped that Galileo will be launched in 1986 or 1987 (it is currently scheduled to launch in STS-61G in May of 1986). The Shuttle will carry Galileo to earth orbit where Titan Centaur boosters will power it out to Jovian space. When it is approximately 100 days from Jupiter, the probe will separate from the Orbiter, slowing very quickly to about two hundred miles per hour. At that point, a parachute will open, allowing the probe to drift slowly down to the planet's surface. It is hoped that Galileo will obtain data explaining Jovian weather, and thus provide insights into earth's weather mechanisms. The Orbiter will relay the probe's data back to earth. It will also obtain high-resolution pictures of the massive planet and its larger moons, gathering information for some twenty months.

The Galileo patch is rectangular in shape. It has a brown overlock border, and is sewn on a blue twill background. The patch illustrates the Galileo probe descending to the Jovian surface, parachute extended. Above, the probe's Orbiter circles the planet, relaying information back to earth. The right-hand portion of the patch is dominated by a representation of Jupiter's surface. It is sewn in varying shades of gold, tan and brown. The project name is embroidered in black with the planet as its background. The probe and its parachute can be seen in the foreground. They are embroidered in gold mylar. The large dish of the Orbiter's antenna points towards the earth. Its inner surface is embroidered in yellow and trimmed in gold mylar. The Galileo patch is not so much beautiful as it is interesting. Its strange color combinations evoke moods not unlike the emotions experienced when viewing photos of Jupiter. The planet seems wild and mad, with its great red spot, ammoniated atmosphere and impenetrable gravity. Galileo's patch evokes these same feelings with its juxtaposition of browns, golds, blues and yellows. This patch belongs in every collection of space emblems.

Many times NASA's contractors on space projects will commission patches to commemorate their participation. This is the case with the GTSI emblem shown here. GTSI is an abbreviation for Grumman Technical Services Incorporated, a division of Grumman Aircraft. GTSI has responsibility for Shuttle payloads, and designed this patch as a symbol of the company's involvement in the Shuttle program. The GTSI and Grumman logos can be seen amid the blast from the Shuttle SRBs. This patch is not available to the general public. It was designed and manufactured for GTSI personnel. It is not an official NASA emblem.

Another example of a contractor's patch is the BSM patch. This patch celebrates the Booster Separation Motor, which is made by the Chemical Systems Division of United Space Boosters, Inc. The BSM consists of eight small rockets, which ignite just prior to SRB shutoff in a Shuttle launch. These small rockets push the SRBs away from the Orbiter and the External Tank, helping to facilitate their successful separation. A typical BSM configuration is depicted at the bottom of the patch. At the top, two SRBs are pushed away from the Shuttle as it climbs into orbit.

The Comet Halley patch is one of the better commemoratives of the comet's return. This patch was first developed and marketed some two years before the famous comet was again visible from earth. It celebrates an astronomical event that will be a once-in-a-lifetime experience for many earthlings of the late twentieth century. The patch depicts the comet with a tail of many hues. At the top, the comet's name is embroidered in light yellow against a black twill background. At the bottom, a clever phrase adds a bit of humor and excitement to the emblem's message.

One of the most puzzling emblems is the mysterious "You've come a long way, baby!" This is not an official NASA emblem, and historians at NASA are unable to explain its significance. The patch is round, with a small cross extending from the lower border. This is the scientific community's symbol for woman (♀).

The center design portrays what appears to be the insignia of a registered nurse, circled by the number 12 inside a white square. At the top, NASA 73 implies some significant event for medical women in NASA that year. Extensive research has produced no answers to the mystery. If any reader is familiar with this patch, the authors would be grateful for any information about its meaning and origins.

12 ▪ NASA FACILITY LOGOS

Every NASA facility has identifying badges and patches which are worn by security personnel and other employees. These are usually rectangular patches, roughly 3″ × 4″, with black lettering embroidered onto an orange background. The Lewis Research Center version depicted here is a typical example. The patch has a white, overlock border surrounding an orange twill background. A large NASA is embroidered in white. Below it, the base name, Lewis Research Center, is sewn in black.

However, some of the NASA facilities have also designed logo-type emblems which are available to collectors and the general public through NASA Visitor Centers and Exchanges.

One of the most sought-after of these patches is the Dryden facility emblem. NASA's Dryden Flight Facility is located at Edwards Air Force Base, prime landing site of the Space Shuttle. The patch is a 4″ diameter, round emblem with a gold overlock border. It depicts the Orbiter making its final turn over the California landscape in preparation for landing. At the top, NASA is embroidered in white. Around the bottom edge Dryden Flight Research Facility is sewn in gold.

NASA's Ames Research Center is located in Northern California, not far from San Francisco. Ames is known extensively for its aerodynamic and wind-tunnel research. Much work on Shuttle and aviation aerodynamics has been done there. The Ames patch is a dome-shaped emblem. It is fully embroidered and has a white, overlock ravel-proof border. A white bar extends across its center, containing a red NASA. Below this, in a field of blue, Ames Research Center is embroidered in white. Above the bar, a space scene depicts a white rocket followed by a contrail. Three white stars complete the scene.

The Jet Propulsion Laboratory in Pasadena, California is known for what its name implies. JPL is also responsible for a number of the planetary probes that have been launched over the years, including the old Project Viking, mission to Mars, and the upcoming Galileo, a Jupiter probe due to be launched in 1986 by the Space Shuttle. The JPL patch is very basic, resembling the NASA worm. The patch is 3½″ × 4″ in size. It has a white twill background with a white overlock border. JPL is embroidered in large red letters in the center. Underneath, in smaller red letters, is the name Jet Propulsion Laboratory.

Lewis Research Center in Cleveland, Ohio has three main areas of responsibility for NASA. They are propulsion, communications and space power. All three are celebrated in the design of the Lewis patch. This is a 4″ diameter, round emblem. It has a light-blue, overlock border. An inner white band exhibits the three aspects of the base: propulsion, communication and space power. All three are sewn in red. The center scene of the patch depicts a communications satellite, a rocket engine and a propulsion system. A center band of white is embroidered with a red NASA worm. Below the logo, the base name and location are sewn in light blue.

The National Space Technology Laboratories

are located in the swamps of Mississippi on the edge of the Louisiana border. NSTL is charged with development, maintenance and production of the Space Shuttle main engines. This is celebrated in the base patch. The patch is a 3" square emblem sewn on an orange twill background. It has a black overlock border. The center scene depicts an alligator dressed in workmen's garb riding on one of the Shuttle main engines. Grasped in his hand is an open-end wrench, and perched on his head is a hardhat. NSTL's full name is embroidered around the worker and his engine. At the top of the entire scene is the base slogan From Swamp to Space embroidered in black. The explanatory Space Shuttle Main Engine is sewn beneath the cartoon.

The Space Port at Kennedy Space Center has developed its own logo, as well. It is a rectangular patch with a white twill background and a white overlock border. Embroidered in red and black at the top are the NASA and Kennedy Space Center's identifiers. Below them the words Space Port follow in the trail of a stylized USA, which is sewn in red, white and blue.

Kennedy Space Center is also the home of a very unusual fireman's patch. The NASA fire and rescue team at Kennedy Space Center wear a traditional firefighter's Maltese Cross emblem. It has an oversewn gold border which surrounds bright red arms of the cross. The inner background of the patch is embroidered in royal blue and contains a view of the Shuttle as seen from above the cargo bay. The Orbiter is sewn in the traditional white with black trim. Surrounding this scene at its edge is the location, John F. Kennedy Space Center. Each part of the cross carries further explanation. At the top, the word NASA is embroidered in gold. The left portion of the cross is embroidered with fire, and the right with rescue. At the bottom are the initials U.S.A.

Sometimes a NASA group or facility will design a patch around a specific event. The NASA facility at Wallops Island, Virginia does not have a base logo patch at this time. However, this facility dates back to the early days of NACA, in 1945. Thus, it was only fitting that the base have a fortieth anniversary emblem created for the 1985 celebration of Wallops Island's involvement in the national Space Program. The patch is hexagonal in shape and is sewn a plum-colored twill background. It has a matching overlock border. At the top, in black embroidery, is the phrase 40th ANNIVERSARY. At the bottom, again in black, is sewn WALLOPS ISLAND, VA. NACA and NASA are sewn on the sides, as are the dates, 1945 and 1985. The center scene has a blue background upon which are four elements of flight known at Wallops: a balloon, an airplane, a rocket, and a dish antenna (for ground station activities). This patch was commissioned for the Visitor's Center at Wallops Island. A limited quantity was made for the anniversary. The best chance for a collector to obtain one is to contact the Wallops Island Visitor's Center on a direct basis.

Even though one always associates spaceflight with NASA, our Space Agency is involved in variety of aeronautics programs as well. Indeed, at Dryden Flight Facility and at Ames Research Center, a great deal of work has been done on the tilt-rotor concept of aircraft development. A tilt-rotor aircraft is one that can literally tilt its engine so that it can take off and hover like a helicopter. Once in flight, the motors can be tilted back into a horizontal position and it will fly like an airplane. Both facilities commissioned patches for the Bell XV-15, an experimental tilt-rotor aircraft built by Bell Helicopter Corporation. The patches are identical except for the base designation. The Dryden version says Dryden/Ames on the patch, and the Ames version simply says Ames. The craft is being developed for NASA, the Army, and the Navy, so all three groups have their name embroidered on the emblems.

Vandenberg Air Force Base will soon be an active Shuttle launch site. While no official logo patches have been developed by Vandenberg, there are any number of unofficial emblems being produced in anticipation of the event. Most have a military flavor, which is predictable since Vandenberg will be the launch site of the military's Shuttle missions. In particular, two of these emblems are worthy of additional note. The first is a triangular emblem, which depicts the Shuttle in launch mode, rising from the California landscape. The words Vandenberg Launch Site are embroidered on the sides and the word Discovery is embroidered at the top.

This patch was made to celebrate the first Vandenberg Shuttle launch, originally scheduled for mid to late 1985. It seems likely that this first launch will be pushed back as late as November or December of 1986 since launch-site preparations and inspections are taking longer than anticipated. The patch will become a better collector's item if this is true, since it would mean that the first Shuttle to be launched from the west coast could be *Atlantis* and not *Discovery*.

The second of the patches worthy of note is the Van D. Berg Space Mechanic patch. This, too, is a souvenir emblem which has enjoyed some popularity on the west coast. It is a humorous depiction of the many workers who have contributed to the construction of Shuttle Launch Complex #6 (SLC-6 or slick 6, as it is known), the Shuttle site at Vandenberg. Van D. Berg is apparently so popular with the workers at Vandenberg that he has appeared on this patch, a number of t-shirts, decals, bumper stickers, and many other products.

13 ■ COLLECTING SPACE PATCHES

Starting Your Collection

You are ready to begin. You've decided that you'd like to personally be a part of the drama and history of the Space Program, by building a personal Space Patch collection.

How do you start? What is the right way to collect? How expensive is it? Where do you find the patches? How do you get in touch with other collectors? How should you keep them? What should you do with them?

Do you only want space shuttle patches? Only the patches of flights which have had significant scientific results? Only moon-related patches? Patches in which certain types of astronauts flew, such as women? Blacks? Non-Americans? Program Patches? Mission Patches? Patches that are not round? Patches that demonstrate design excellence? Only official patches? All patches? In collecting space patches as in the space program, itself, the only rule should be: Do not impose any limitations or barriers on your imagination.

The good news is that there is no "right" way to collect patches. Design your own collection and base it on your own interests. Collect to suit your desires! You will find a world of knowledge and beauty opening up to you. Your collection will grow as your interests grow. Your enjoyment and appreciation of the patches will broaden your knowledge of America, embroidery, art, space and science.

You will find yourself getting "involved" in your collection. You will be anxious to show off your collection as well as to share your growing knowledge. You will try to read more and study more. (The books listed in the bibliography will help you as you find yourself getting more interested in our space program.) The collection should not be the end in itself; let it be the beginning of a journey of understanding the successes and failures of all aspects of human achievement. Let it make a difference in your own life just as space exploration has made a difference in everyone's life.

APPENDICES

TIMELINE
Mercury Manned Flights

SPACECRAFT	LAUNCH DATE	CREW	REVOLUTIONS	DURATION	DETAILS
Mercury 3	5/5/61	Alan Shepard	suborbital	15 mins	1st American in space
Mercury 4	7/21/61	Virgil Grissom	suborbital	15 mins	capsule sank
Mercury 6	2/20/62	John Glenn	3	4 hrs 55 mins	1st American in orbit
Mercury 7	5/24/62	Scott Carpenter	3	4 hrs 56 mins	250 mile overshoot
Mercury 8	10/3/62	Walter Schirra	6	9 hrs 13 mins	landed on target
Mercury 9	5/15/63	Gordon Cooper	22	1 day 10 hrs 20 mins	1st long flight by U.S.

Gemini Missions

SPACECRAFT	LAUNCH DATE	CREW	REVOLUTIONS	DURATION	DETAILS
Gemini 3	3/23/65	Virgil Grissom, John Young	3	4 hrs 53 mins	1st orbital maneuvers
Gemini 4	6/3/65	James McDivitt, Ed White	62	4 days 1 hr 56 mins	1st spacewalk
Gemini 5	8/21/65	Gordon Cooper, Pete Conrad	120	7 days 22 hrs 56 mins	1st extended manned flight
Gemini 7	12/4/65	Frank Borman, James Lovell	206	13 days 18 hrs 35 mins	Longest U.S. flight for 8 years
Gemini 6	12/15/65	Walter Schirra, Thomas Stafford	16	1 day 1 hr 51 mins	Rendezvous to 6' Gemini 7
Gemini 8	3/16/66	Neil Armstrong, David Scott	6	10 hrs 41 mins	1st docking emergency splashdown

Gemini (continued)

Gemini 9	6/3/66	Thomas Stafford Eugene Cernan	45	3 days 0 hrs 21 mins	2 hour space walk (Cernan)
Gemini 10	7/18/66	John Young Michael Collins	43	2 days 22 hrs 47 mins	Rendezvous with 2 targets
Gemini 11	9/12/66	Pete Conrad Richard Gordon	44	2 days 23 hrs 17 mins	Rendezvous & docking
Gemini 12	11/11/66	James Lovell Edwin Aldrin	59	3 days 22 hrs 34 mins	Dockings & 3 spacewalks

Apollo Missions

SPACECRAFT	DATE	CREW	REVOLUTIONS	DURATION	DETAILS
Apollo 1	None	Gus Grissom Ed White Roger Chaffee	None	None	Crew die in fire on pad
Apollo 7	10/11/68	Walt Schirra Donn Eisele Walt Cunningham	163	10 days 20 hrs 9 mins	1st manned Apollo flight
Apollo 8	12/21/68	Frank Borman Jim Lovell Bill Anders	10 Lunar Revs	6 days 3 hrs 0 mins	1st manned flight around moon
Apollo 9	3/3/69	Jim McDivitt David Scott Russ Schweickart	151	10 days 1 hrs 1 min	Dock with LEM
Apollo 10	5/18/69	Tom Stafford Gene Cernan John Young	31 Lunar Revs	8 days 0 hours 3 mins	Dress Rehearsal
Apollo 11	7/16/69	Neil Armstrong "Buzz" Aldrin Mike Collins	31 *CML Revs	8 days 3 hrs 18 mins	1st manned lunar landing
Apollo 12	11/14/69	Charles Conrad Dick Gordon Alan Bean	49 CML Revs	10 days 4 hrs 36 mins	Lightning strike at launch
Apollo 13	4/11/70	Jim Lovell John Swigert Fred Haise	None	5 days 22 hrs 55 mins	Abort; 1st space rescue
Apollo 14	1/31/71	Alan Shepard Stuart Roosa Ed Mitchell	34 CML Revs	9 days 0 hrs 42 mins	Golf on lunar surface

Apollo 15	7/26/71	David Scott James Irwin Al Worden	74 CML Revs	12 days 7 hrs 12 mins	1st use of lunar Rover
Apollo 16	4/16/72	John Young Ken Mattingly Charles Duke	64 CML Revs	11 days 1 hr 51 mins	3 EVA's
Apollo 17	12/6/72	Gene Cernan Ron Evans H. Schmitt	75 CML Revs	12 days 13 hrs 51 mins	Last and longest moon flight

*CML Revs are Command Module Lunar Revolutions

Skylab Missions

SPACECRAFT	LAUNCH DATE	CREW	REVOLUTIONS	DURATION	DETAILS
Skylab	5/14/73	Unmanned	34,981		Vibration during liftoff
Skylab 1	5/25/73	Charles Conrad Joseph Kerwin Paul Weitz	404	28 days 0 hrs 50 mins	EVA's repair damage
Skylab 2	7/28/73	Alan Bean Owen Garriott Jack Lousma	858	59 days 11 hrs 9 mins	Rescue prepared not needed
Skylab 3	11/16/73	Gerald Carr Ed Gibson Bill Pogue	1,214	84 days 1 hr 15 mins	Total EVA's 82 hrs 47 mins

Apollo/Soyuz

SPACECRAFT	LAUNCH DATE	CREW	REVOLUTIONS	DURATION	DETAILS
ASTP	7/15/75	Tom Stafford Vance Brand Deke Slayton	138	9 days 1 hr 28 mins	1st US/ SOVIET joint flight docked 43 hrs

INDEX

A.B. Emblem Company, 35
Acton, Loren, 92
Agena rocket, 42
Aldrin, Edwin (Buzzy), Jr., 46, 52
Allen, Joseph, 76, 77, 88
Al-Saud, Sultan bin Salman, 91
Ames patch, 114
Ames Research Center, 114, 115
Anders, Bill, 49, 50
Anderson, Jack, 107
Anik C, 79
Anik C-1, 89
Anik C-3, 76–77
Anik D2, 87
Apollo 11, Lem 5 patch, 19, 54
Apollo Lunar Surface Experiment Package (ALSEP), 55
"Apollo Moonscape," 53–54
Apollo Program, 9–11, 47–60, 122–123
  Apollo 1, 9, 48–49
  Apollo 4, 49
  Apollo 5, 49
  Apollo 6, 49
  Apollo 7, 9, 49
  Apollo 8, 9, 49–50
  Apollo 9, 9, 49, 50
  Apollo 10, 10, 51
  Apollo 11, 10, 51–54
  Apollo 12, 10, 54–55
  Apollo 13, 10, 55–56
  Apollo 14, 10, 56–58
  Apollo 15, 11, 58–59
  Apollo 16, 11, 59
  Apollo 17, 11, 59–60

  goals, 47
  program patch, 11, 47–48
Apollo/Soyuz Test Program, 11, 66–68, 123
Approach and Landing Tests (ALT), 13, 70–71
Ariane patch, ESA, 103
Ariane rocket, 70
Armstrong, Neil, 44, 52
Army Institute of Heraldry, 38
Astronaut pin, 57
Astronet, 108
"Astronomical glitch" on Apollo 11 patch, 53
Atlantis, 70, 72
  STS-51J, 93–94
  STS-61B, 94–95
Atlas-D booster, 39
Aurora 7, 41

Bales, Steve, 52
Bartoe, John-David, 92
Bassett, Charles, II, 45
Baudry, Patrick, 91, 106
Bean, Al, 54, 55, 63
Beep Beep patch, 19, 57–58
Bell XV-15 patch, 115
Black worm patch, 5, 38
Bluford, Guion, 80–82, 94
Bobko, Karol, 78, 90, 93
Bolden, Charles, 95
Booster Separation Motor (BSM), 113
Borders, 37
Borman, Frank, 44, 49, 50
Brand, Vance, 66, 76, 84
Brandenstein, Daniel, 80, 82, 91

Brezhnev, Leonid, 67
Bridges, Roy, Jr., 92
BSM patch, 32, 113
Buchli, James F., 88, 94
Burson, Harold, 107
Bush, George, 96

CANADARM, 73, 74, 87, 105–106
  patch, 24, 105–106
Canadian Astronaut Program, 24, 35, 105–106
  Anik C, 79
  Anik C-1, 89
  Anik C-3, 76–77
  Anik D2, 87
  Young Astronauts Program, 21, 107
Canadian Shuttle Mission Patch, 25, 106
Carpenter, Scott, 40–41
Carr, Gerald, 64
Cenker, Robert, 95
Cernan, Eugene, 45, 51, 57, 59
CFES experiment, 75, 80, 81, 89–90
Chaffee, Roger, 48
Challenger, 70, 72, 75–76, 78–86
  STS-6, 78–79
  STS-7, 79–80
  STS-8, 80–82
  STS-11 (STS-41B), 83–85
  STS-41C, 85–86
  STS-41G, 86–87, 106
  STS-51B, 90–91
  STS-51E, 89
  STS-51F, 92–93

STS-51G, 91–92
STS-51L, 96–98
STS-61A, 94
Chang-Diaz, Franklin, 95
Charlie Brown, 51
Chretien, Jean-Loup, 106
Cleave, Mary, 94
Coats, Michael, 86
Collecting space patches, 35, 117
Collins, Michael, 45, 50
Colors, 35
Columbia, 52, 70, 72–78
    STS-1, 13, 72–73
    STS-2, 13, 73–74
    STS-3, 14, 74–75
    STS-4, 14, 75–76
    STS-5, 14, 76–78
    STS-9, 15, 82–83
    STS-61C, 95–96
Columbiad, 50
Comet Halley patch, 113
Commemorative emblem, Apollo 11, 19, 53–54
Computer, embroidery by, 34
Conrad, Charles, 62
Conrad, Pete, 43, 45–46, 54, 55
Constitution, 70
Continuous filament rayon threads, 35
Continuous Flow Electrophoresis System (CFES), 75, 80, 81, 89–90
Cook, Captain, 90
Cooper, Gordon, 41, 43
Covey, Richard, 93
Creighton, John, 91
Crests, 34
Crew patches of Apollo/Soyuz mission, 68
Crippen, Robert, 72, 79, 85–87
Cryogenic Infra-red Radiance Telescope (Cirris), 75
Cunningham, Walter, 49

da Vinci, Leonardo, 63, 64, 106
Designs, changes in, 33
Diffusive Mixings of Organic Solutions (DMOS) experiment, 87–88

Discovery, 70, 72
    STS-41D, 15, 86
    STS-51A, 16, 87–88
    STS-51C, 16, 88–89
    STS-51D, 16, 89–90
    STS-51G, 17, 106
    STS-51I, 17, 93
Downs, Hugh, 107
Dryden Flight Facility, 114, 115
    emblem, 26, 114
Duke, Charles, 59
Dunbar, Bonnie, 94

Eagle, 52, 53
Earthnet emblem, ESA, 104–105
Earth Radiation Budget Satellite (ERBS), 87
Eisele, Donn, 49
Embroidery
    defined, 34
    history of, 34–36
England, Anthony, 92
Engle, Joe, 57, 71, 73, 93
Enos the chimp, 40
Enterprise (OV-101), 70–71
ERBS, 87
Eureca (European Retrieval Carrier) 22, 104
European Space Agency (ESA), 82
    Ariane rocket, 70
    patches, 103–105
Evans, Ron, 57, 59
Extended Vector, NASA, 38

Fabian, Norman John, 79, 91
Fabric, basic, 35
Facility logos, NASA, 114–116
Faith 7, 41
Falcon, 58
"Fineness of resolution," 34
Fireman's patch, Kennedy Space Center, 27, 115
First Lunar Landing emblems, 19, 54
Fisher, Anna, 88, 93
Fisher, William (Bill), 93
Fletcher, James, 70
Ford, Gerald, 67, 70
Freas, Kelly, 62

Freedom 7, 39, 40
French astronauts, 106
French Echocardiograph Experiment (FEE), 91, 106
French Postural Experiment, 91, 106
Friendship 7, 40
From the Earth to the Moon (Verne), 50
Fullerton, Gordon, 71, 74, 75, 92
Furrer, Reinhard, 94

Gagarin, Yuri, 72
Galileo patch, 31, 112–113
Gardner, Dale, 80–82, 88
Garn, Jake, 90, 95, 101
Garneau, Marc, 86, 87, 105, 106
Garn patch, 17, 101
Garriott, Owen, 63, 82, 83
Gemini program, 7–8, 42–46, 121–122
    Gemini 3, 7, 42–43
    Gemini 4, 7, 43
    Gemini 5, 7, 43
    Gemini 6, 7, 44
    Gemini 7, 7, 43–44
    Gemini 8, 8, 44–45
    Gemini 9, 8, 45
    Gemini 10, 8, 45
    Gemini 11, 8, 45–46
    Gemini 12, 8, 46
Genesis Rock, 58
Get Away Specials, 75, 77, 87
    patch, 99
Gibson, Ed, 64
Gibson, Robert "Hoot," 84, 95
Glenn, John, 40
Gordon, Richard, Jr., 45–46, 54, 55
GPS NAVSTAR patch, 30, 111
Grabe, Ronald, 93
Gregory, Frederick, 90
Griggs, David, 90
Grissom, Virgil, 40, 42, 48
Grumman Technical Services Incorporated (GTSI) emblem, 32, 113

Hadley Rille, 58

Haise, Fred, 55, 71
Halley comet patch, 113
Ham the chimpanzee, 39
Hart, Terry, 85
Hartsfield, Henry, 75, 76, 86, 94
Hauck, Frederick, 79, 88
Hawley, Steven, 86, 95
Henize, Karl, 92
Hilmers, David, 93
Hoffman, Jeffrey, 90
Hubble, Edwin P., 112
Hubble Space Telescope patch, 31, 112
Hudson, Henry, 90

"I Love NASA" emblem, 5, 38
Indian National Satellite INSAT-1B, 80, 81
Indonesia's Palapa B communications satellite, 79–80, 84, 87
Inertial Upper Stage (IUS), 78
Insignias, 34
International space patches, 22–25, 103–106
    Canadian Astronaut Program, 24, 105–106
    European Space Agency, 22–23, 103–105
    French astronauts, 106
Intrepid, 54, 55
Irregulier style border, 37
Irwin, Jim, 58

Jarvis, Gregory B., 96, 97
Jet Propulsion Laboratory (JPL) patch, 26, 114
Johnson & Johnson, 89
J Series missions, 58

Kennedy, John F., 47
Kennedy Space Center fireman's patch, 27, 115
Kerwin, Joseph, 62
Kohoutek, 64
Kosygin, A., 66
Kraft, Chris, 59
Kubasov, Valeri, 66

LDEF, 85, 99–100

LEASAT 1 (SYNCOM IV-1), 87
LEASAT 3 satellite, 89
Leestma, David, 86
Lenoir, William, 76, 77
Leonov, Alexei, 66
Lewis Research Center patch, 26, 114
Liberty Bell 7, 40
Lichtenbert, Byron, 82, 83
Lind, Carol Ann, 91
Lind, Don, 91
Logos
    Canadian Astronaut Program, 24, 105
    NASA, 37–38
    NASA facility, 114–116
Long Duration Exposure Facility (LDEF), 85, 99–100
    patch, 31, 100
Lounge, John, 93
Lousma, Jack, 63, 74, 75
Lovell, James, 44, 46, 49, 50, 55
Lucid, Shannon, 91
Lunar Project Apollo. *See* Apollo Program
Lunar Rover, 58, 60

Machine embroidery, 34
Manned Maneuvering Unit (MMU), 84
    patch, 30, 100–101
Mattingly, Ken, 59, 75, 76, 88
Mattingly, Tom, 55
McAuliffe, Sharon Christa, 96, 107, 111–112
McBride, John A., 86
McCall, Robert C., 75
McCandless, Bruce, 84
McDivitt, James, 43, 50
McDonnell Douglas Astronautics Co., 75, 80, 89
McNair, Ronald E., 84, 96, 97
"Meatball" patch, 38
Merbold, Ulf, 82, 83
Mercury program, 6, 39–41, 121
    Mercury-Atlas 1 to 4, 39
    Mercury-Atlas 5, 40
    Mercury-Atlas 6, 40

Mercury-Atlas 7, 40–41
Mercury-Atlas 8, 41
Mercury-Atlas 9, 41
Mercury-Redstone 1, 39
Mercury-Redstone 2, 39
Mercury-Redstone 3, 39
Mercury-Redstone 4, 40
Mercury 3 patch, 6, 39–40
Messerschmid, Ernst, 94
Mission Control Team Emblem, 32, 101–102
Mitchell, Ed, 56, 57
MMU, 84, 100–101
Molly Brown, 42, 43
Moon landings, 47, 52–60
Morgan, Barbara R., 97
Mullane, Richard, 86
Musgrave, Story, 78, 92

NACA patch, 5, 37
Nagel, Steven, 91, 94
Nagy, Alex, 42
NASA
    anniversary patch, 26, 110
    extended vector, 5, 38
    facility logos, 114–116
    logos, 5, 37–38
    original patch, 5, 37
    "worm," 5, 38
National Advisory Committee on Aeronautics, 5, 37
National Space Technology Laboratories (NSTL), 114–115
    patch, 115
Navstar Global Positioning System (GPS NAVSTAR), 30, 111
Nelson, Bill, 95
Nelson, George, 85, 95
Neri, Rudolpho, 95
Nixon, Richard M., 52, 66

Ockels, Wubbo, 94
O'Connor, Bryan, 94
Office of Aeronautics and Space Technology (OAST)
OAST-1, 86
OAST-1 patch, 100
Office of Space and Terrestrial Applications (OSTA)

OSTA-1, 31, 73
OSTA-2, 80
OSTA-3, 87
Office of Space Science and Applications. *See* Office of Space and Terrestrial Applications (OSTA)
Olympus 1, 104
Onizuka, Ellison, 88, 96, 97
Oscillations, pogo, 49
Overlock style border, 37
Overmyer, Robert, 76, 77, 90

Pailes, William, 93
Palapa B communication satellites, 79–80, 84, 87
Pantone Matching System (PMS), 35
Parker, Robert, 82, 83
Patch, use of term, 34
Payton, Gary E., 88
Peterson, Donald, 78
Physical Vapor Transport of Organic Solids (PVTOS) experiment, 93
Pioneer 10 patch, 32, 110
Podsiadly, Chris, 88
Pogue, William, 64
Program patches
  Apollo/Soyuz missions, 67–68
  Space Shuttle Program, 71
Project Viking, 110–111
Pucci, Emilio, 58
PVTOS, 93

Quality, factors in evaluating, 35

Rawlings, Patrick, 87
Reagan, Ronald, 75, 97, 107
Remote Manipulator System (RMS), 73, 74, 87, 105–106
Rescue mission, Apollo 13 as first space, 56
Resnik, Judith A., 96, 97
Ride, Sally, 73, 79, 80, 86
Rockwell International Corporation, 70
Roosa, Stuart, 56
Ross, Jerry, 94

Salyut missions, 68
  Salyut 7, 76, 106
Satcom Ku-1, 95
Satellite Business System's SBS-3, 76
Saturn 1B, 62, 64, 67
Saturn 5, 54, 61
Savitskaya, Svetlana, 87
Schirra, Walter, 41, 44, 49
Schmitt, Jack, 60
Schulman, Bob, 112
Schweickhart, Russell, 50
Scobee, Francis R. "Dick," 85, 96, 97
Scott, David, 44, 50, 58
Scully-Power, Paul, 86
Sea of Tranquillity, 52
Seddon, Rhea, 90
See, Elliot, 45
Shaw, Brewster, Jr., 82, 83, 94
Shepard, Alan, 39, 40, 47, 56–57
Shriver, Loren J., 88
Shuttle Carriers of America patch, 29, 99
Shuttle Chase Team patch, 29, 99
Shuttle Pallet Satellite (SPAS), 80
Shuttle Transportation System (STS). *See* Space Shuttle Program
Shuttle Triangle, 71–72
Sigma 7, 41
Skylab Program, 12, 61–65, 123
  Skylab I, 12, 62–63
  Skylab II, 12, 63–64
  Skylab 3, 12, 64–65
  thermal shield, 61
Skylab USA, 62
Slayton, Deke, 66
Small Self-Contained Payloads, 75, 77, 87
  emblem, 99
Smith, Michael J., 96, 97
Snoopy, 51
Solar Array, 86
Solar Maximum satellite, 84, 85
Solid Rocket Boosters (SRB), 70, 72

Souvenir versions of patches
  Apollo 1, 48–49
  Apollo 7, 49
  Apollo 8, 50
  Apollo 9, 51
  Apollo 10, 51
  Apollo 11, 53
  Apollo 12, 55
  Apollo 13, 56
  Apollo 14, 57
  Apollo 15, 59
  Apollo 16, 59
  Apollo 17, 60
  Apollo/Soyuz mission, 67
  facility logos, 115–116
  Mercury program, 39–41
  NASA logo, 38
  Shuttle Program, 71–72
  Skylab I, 63
  Skylab II, 64
  Skylab 3, 65
  STS-1, 72–73
  STS-2, 74
  STS-3, 75
  STS-4, 76
  STS-5, 77–78
  STS-7, 79, 80
  STS-41B, 85
  STS-41C, 86
  STS-41D, 86
  STS-41G, 87
  STS-51A, 88
  STS-51C, 89
  STS-51D, 90
  STS-51E, 89
  STS-51F, 92–93
  STS-51I, 93
  STS-51J, 94
  STS-61A, 94
  STS-61C, 96
Soviet Union
  Apollo/Soyuz Test Program, 66–68
  commercial space program, 70
Sputnik, 47
Soyuz 13, 64
Soyuz 19, 67
Soyuz T-6, 106
Space Flight Participant patch, 111–112

Spacelab I, 82–83
  patch, 103–104
Spacelab 2, 92–93
  patch, 104
Spacelab 3, 90
  patch, 104
Spacelab D-1, 94
Spacelab Program patch, ESA, 103
Space Port patch, 115
Space race, 47
Space Shuttle Canadian Astronaut emblem, 105
Space Shuttle Program, 13, 69–98
  Atlantis
    STS-51J, 93–94
    STS-61B, 94–95
  Challenger, 70, 72, 75–76, 78–86
    STS-6, 14, 78–79
    STS-7, 14, 79–80
    STS-8, 15, 80–82
    STS-11 (STS-41B), 83–85
    STS-41C, 85–86
    STS-41G, 86–87, 106
    STS-51B, 90–91
    STS-51E, 89
    STS-51F, 92–93
    STS-51G, 91–92
    STS-51L, 96–98
    STS-61A, 94
  Columbia, 52, 70, 72–78
    STS-1, 13, 72–73
    STS-2, 13, 73–74
    STS-3, 14, 74–75
    STS-4, 14, 75–76
    STS-5, 14, 76–78
    STS-9, 15, 82–83
    STS-61C, 95–96
  Discovery
    STS-41D, 86

    STS-51A, 87–88
    STS-51C, 88–89
    STS-51D, 89–90
    STS-51G, 106
    STS-51I, 93
  Enterprise, 70–71
    origins of, 69
    program patch, 71–72
    "related" patches, 99–102
    size of Shuttle Orbiters, 69–70
Space Telescope patch, ESA, 104
Space to Grow emblem, 101
Spartan astronomy platform, 91
Spartan-Halley Experiment Package, 97
Spring, Sherwood, 94
Sputnik, 47
Stafford, Thomas, 44, 45, 51, 66
Stewart, Robert, 84, 93
STS. *See* Space Shuttle Program
Sullivan, Kathryn D., 86, 87
Surveyor 3, 54–55
Swigert, Jack, 55
Swiss embroidery, 34

TDRSS patch, 100
Thagard, Norman, 79, 90
Thermal shield, Skylab's, 61
Thornton, William, 80, 82, 90
Threads, continuous filament rayon, 35
3M Corporation, 87–88, 93
Titan 2 rockets, 42
Tracking and Data Relay Satellite, 89
  TDRS-A, 78
  TDRS-B, 97

  TDRS-1, 81
Trimming, 35
Truly, Richard, 71, 73, 80, 81–82
25 MACH patch, 102
Twenty-Second Space Congress (1985), 88

Unofficial patch, Apollo 14, 57
  See also Souvenir versions of patches

Van D. Berg Space Mechanic patch, 116
van den Berg, Lodewijk, 90
Vandenberg Air Force Base, 84
  patches, 28, 115–116
van Hoften, James, 85, 93
Verne, Jules, 50
Viking patch, 29, 111
Voyager patch, 29, 111

Walker, Charles, 80, 86, 90, 95
Walker, David, 88
Wallop Island patch, 27, 115
Wang, Taylor, 90
Webb, James E., 43
Weitz, Paul, 62, 78
WESTAR VI, 84, 87
White, Ed, 43, 48
Williams, C.C., 55
Williams, Donald, 90
Worden, Al, 58
Worm logo, 38

Yankee Clipper, 54, 55
Young, John, 42, 45, 59, 72, 82, 83
Young Astronauts Program, 35, 107–109
"You've come a long way, baby!" patch, 30, 113